Charlie's Lab

CHARLIE'S LAB

MICHAEL
S.A. GRAZIANO

Press 53
Winston-Salem

Press 53, LLC
PO Box 30314
Winston-Salem, NC 27130

First Edition

Press 53 Immersion Series
Edited by Christopher Forrest

Cover art, "Origami Puzzle Monkey," by AnaBi
Licensed through Adobe Stock

Cover design by Claire V. Foxx

Library of Congress Control Number
2023932508

ISBN 978-1-950413-64-5

CONTENTS

Introduction   vii

The Entrance   5
Corridor A   7
Corridor B, West Wall   12
Corridor B, North End   28
Corridor B, East Wall   32
The Lunchroom   42
The Awake Room   50
The Quarantine Room   61
The Prep Room   63
The Computer Room   75
The Darkroom   77
The Histology Room   79
The Surgery Room   89
Three Little Rooms   95
The Baby Room   97
The Black Hole   100
Dylan's Office   103
The Colony: Heart of the Lab   106
My Perfect Office   112
Maida's Office   117
Charlie's Office: Soul of the Lab   119
Tirin's Office   124
The Kitchen and the Shop   126
The Last Little Room   132
Exodus   133

About the Author   137

INTRODUCTION

Behind me, in the immense, crowded, central hall of the DC convention center, I hear my name booming out of the background din of voices. "Michael! Michael! I found you a woman!"

I turn around. Thirty feet away, pushing through the crowd, Charlie Gross is stumping along in his slightly off-kilter mode of ambulation, one arm clutching a canvas sack with books and papers, the other hand up and waving vigorously at me. His dark, long, wavy hair is flying around his head, his white beard bristling and flashing, his deeply tanned, wrinkled face stretching and puckering around his eyes in intense excitement. "Michael! Eat lunch with me! I found you a woman!"

I'm acutely embarrassed. In the 1990s, you can't just blurt out stuff like that. Charlie is ethically unimpeachable, egalitarian, and feminist, but also anti-establishment and anti-boring. He acts and speaks in his own way.

What he means, I find out as we sit at a noisy café in the main conference hall, is that in a kind of orgasm of gregarious enthusiasm at this annual Society for Neuroscience conference, he's found a potential collaborator for my experiments on auditory space. The fact that the collaborator is an intelligent and successful woman seems to have sparked a matchmaking joy in him. Some of his outburst is probably showmanship, but I think most of it is a childlike enthusiasm and warmth, oblivious to stares and embarrassment, combined with a vivid sense of humor. Charlie takes his science seriously and he takes his people seriously, but he rarely takes himself so. Charlie out in the wild is the same as Charlie at home in the lab. He is who he is. Extravagant, strange, brilliant, and lovely.

Charlie is arguably the most successful neuroscience mentor of the twentieth century, more movers and shakers having come out of his lab than any other. But we students come out reluctantly. When we do venture out and try other jobs, we don't stay away for long. We come running back to spend another few years, desperate to remain within his sphere of influence. He is the Socrates of cognitive neuroscience, not just because of his shaggy beard and sandals, or because of his own creativity, but because of his influence on the world through his halo of students. He taught us how to ask insightful questions unencumbered by the latest group-think.

Charlie Gross grew up in Brooklyn, New York, in the 1930s. His parents, who belonged to the US Communist party, carefully hid their political activities from their son in order to protect him from stigma. But they must have given him some of their left political energy: a deep suspicion of authority, a preference for anything counterculture, and a belief in social fairness. In his early school years, his teachers repeatedly shamed him for his disruptive energy, his impulsive talking in class, his stutter, and his shaky, left-handed writing. The shaming might have helped stoke his anti-authority, anarchistic personality. None of it held him back. In high school, he performed brilliantly in his history and science classes, and won a coveted Westinghouse Science Talent Search award, one of the highest honors in the country, for an experiment in botany. He also became an Eagle Scout, for which he felt so proud that he listed it on his curriculum vitae for the rest of his life. And no matter where he went after high school, despite all the people and cultures he encountered, he never lost his thick, Jewish Brooklyn accent. He had, as he said, a tin ear.

Working at Cambridge, MIT, Harvard, and eventually settling at Princeton, he focused his scientific career on the study of the primate brain. His early experiments tracked the effects of damage to the cerebral cortex. He then moved to the more refined technique of measuring the electrical signals in individual neurons, listening in on the brain as it talked to itself. He's probably most famous for discovering specific neurons that act as face detectors, the so-called face cells in the temporal cortex that allow you to recognize your mom, your friends, your favorite celebrities. Discoveries like these, not little incremental advances but Charlie's inspired leaps of insight, seemingly so effortless, so out-of-the-blue, opened up a whole field of study. Cognitive neuroscience, it's now called. When Charlie first started his work, neuroscience was as far from exploring meaningful human cognition as, say, a bicycle is from exploring outer space. Now, many decades later, studying the neural basis of higher cognition is the rage everywhere. Charlie showed that it was possible. I can't think of any neuroscientist in the second half of the twentieth century who had a bigger impact, although some may have won fancier prizes. Charlie's work, always countercultural, always outside of people's comfortable mental boxes, was never calculated to win prizes.

He built his Princeton lab in 1970. I arrived in 1987, and stayed until the place was torn down in 2002. During its thirty-two years, the lab was not just one of the world's hotspots of science, but it was also our home. We lived there embedded in a transparent gel of intellectual idealism, a manifestation of Charlie's personality. We grew up in that place, ate our meals there, entertained ourselves, sometimes slept the night, and even had internal lab romances. We spent far more time in it than out of it. I can see every bit of the lab so vividly in my mind that it feels like it must still exist in some Platonic world of the abstract. Sometimes you spend so long in a place that you never leave it, and Charlie's lab is where my intellectual heart is.

In 2019, when I heard that Charlie was in Hospice care, not fully aware of his surroundings and in his last days, I didn't know how to react, but I suddenly and very badly wanted to go back to the old lab. I wanted to walk around, sit in the familiar chairs, look at the lovely chaotic clutter—the intellectual mulch of the place—and feel Charlie's presence holding us together. I had such an aching for the old lab that I didn't know what to do. It was gone—torn down seventeen years previously.

If I were at the top of the *Forbes* list and had a few billion dollars to spare, I guess I'd rebuild the place one authentic detail at a time and open a museum. A lot of us have taken pieces of the old lab home for remembrances—especially the colored toilet brushes and plastic lizards that were once used as visual stimuli to probe the brain's responses. But maybe I don't need artifacts or a billion dollars. I can rebuild the place with words, and my written museum will be more durable and accurate than any brick-and-mortar version could be.

The human eye makes fast, saccadic movements about three times a second, as Charlie could have told you, and every time the eye lands, it picks out a tiny circle of focused detail. It might register the shape of a doorknob or the color of a light switch. Your understanding of a room or a mood or a personality or an epoch of your life is stitched together out of tiny, vivid fragments. That's how I want to recreate the lab—through a million meticulous details. I want to immerse you in the place.

Sure, I'll put in stories—adventures that happened to us in that world—and running underneath them all, I think, will be the story of time, the story of how things change and end. Or maybe my book is an attempt to stop things from changing and ending. But I give fair warning: I'm intentionally going to throw away most of what an author is supposed to know about the craft. I'm aware this project is no exciting action plot or character portrait. It's not a biography either. It doesn't fit the standard forms. It's about a place rather than a person, except the place is the person, and the person is rarely mentioned, and the stories are mainly about other people, and about doorknobs and colors and sounds and smells and scientific equipment and also, somehow, always about the man who opened up that space in the universe and presided over it for three decades. None of that makes sense; but it does. I think it does. I wouldn't feel morally comfortable, anyway, writing a standard book about someone as fundamentally out-of-the-box as Charlie Gross.

Charlie's Lab

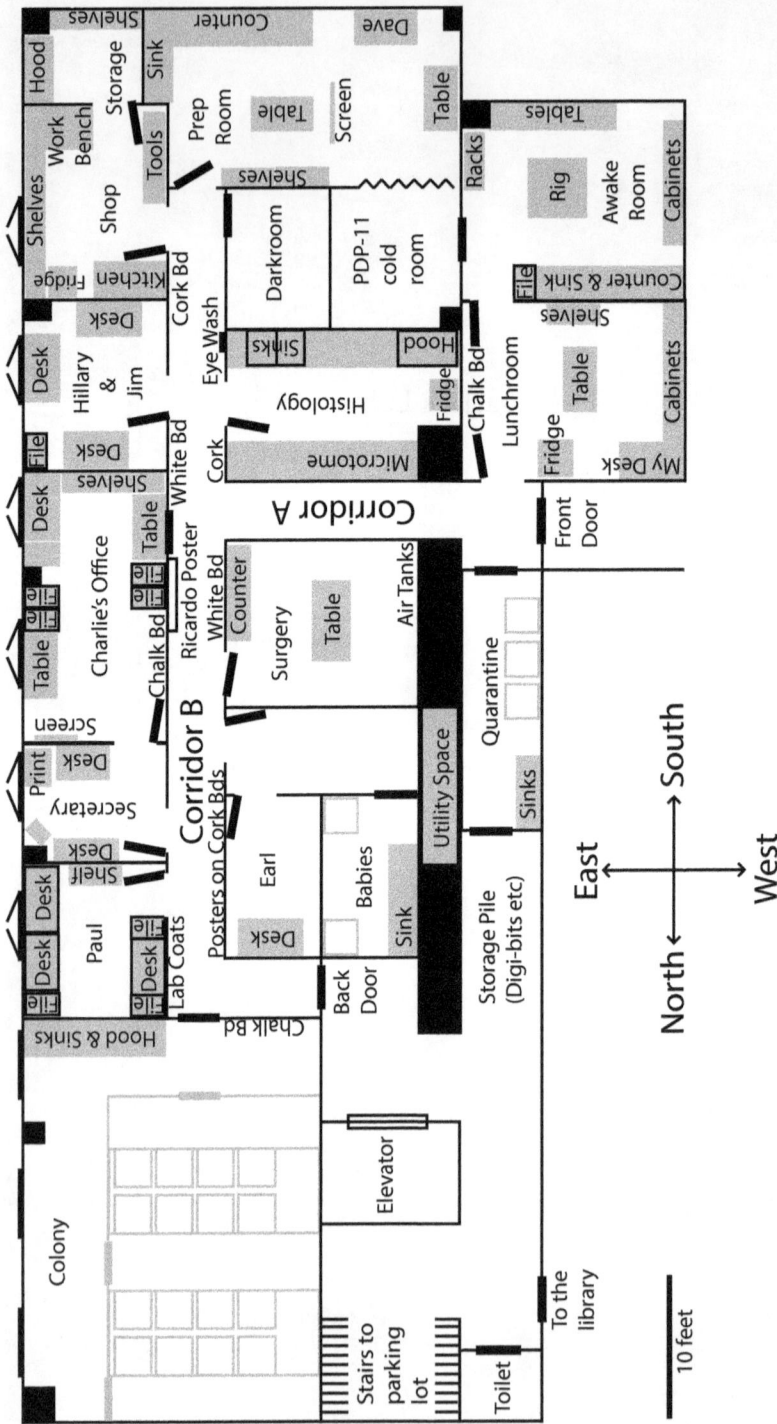

Figure 1. Charlie's Lab in 1987, when I arrived. The walls are indicated by thin black lines, the doors (most of them shown open) by thicker line segments. The double windows along the east wall (at the top) are shown angled partly open, except for those in the monkey colony, which were always bolted shut. The gray rectangles are furniture and the thin gray lines in the colony show the caging that housed the animals. The larger black squares and rectangles are structural pillars and plumbing spaces. The lab encompassed about 3,500 square feet.

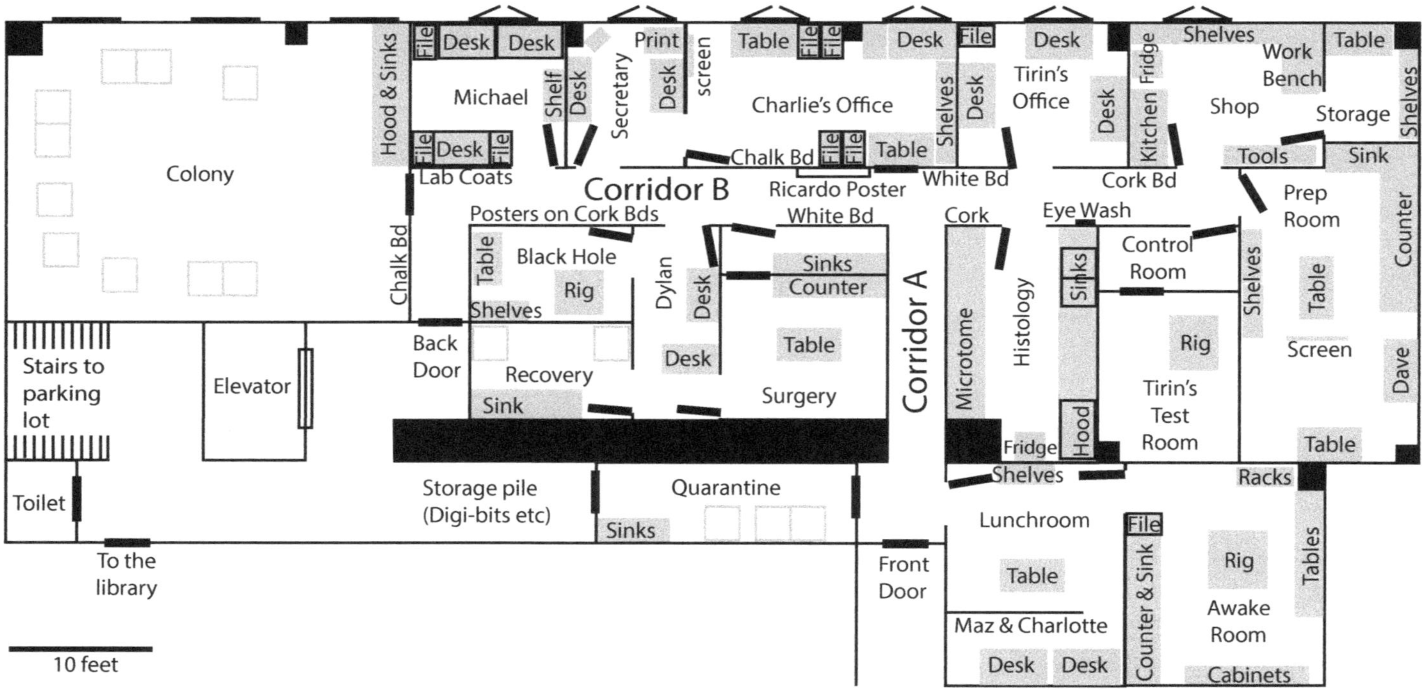

Figure 2. Charlie's Lab in 2002, just before it was torn down. A few walls and details changed over the years, such as the rebuilt surgery.

1

THE ENTRANCE

You stand in a small vestibule, poorly lit, with a notably dirty, linoleum floor. You're facing locked double doors, the blue metal doors to the east wing of the building. While you wait, you peer in through round porthole windows. All you see is a long, dingy corridor. Without special knowledge, you'd have no idea that anything unusual is hidden here. Many labs, many worlds, are packed away in the east wing. You call on an intercom—a beige plastic telephone mounted on the wall just to the right of the doors—pressing 1 for Charlie Gross's lab. If someone lets you in, or you have the 46 key to help yourself, you can walk down the corridor, passing the entrances to other labs, until finally, at the end of the hallway, you reach the door to our own lab. Past moat and portcullis, you're about to walk into our world.

Our front door is new. We didn't used to have a private door separating us from the other labs, and that memory of doorlessness is unsettling to me. Imagine if you lived in an apartment building and your private household had no locked front door, only an open passage connecting directly to the other households—and your neighbors, most of whom you don't know, could walk in any time and steal the yogurt out of your fridge.

A good front door should be protective but also welcoming. Ours is made of warm, brown, varnished wood. It has a silvery lever handle on the left side. The upper half of the door contains a round window, perhaps two feet across, with a crosshatched pattern of wire embedded in the glass. The wire-reinforced porthole is weirdly forbidding and welcoming at the same time. In the middle of the glass, partially blocking your view, a messy sign has been posted, a sideways piece of printer paper crinkled and stuffed into a clear plastic sleeve, taped loosely to the glass with four pieces of bright yellow tape.

Typical of any sign posted where you can see it every day, whatever urgent message it's meant to convey, I can't remember a word of it, because I never pay attention. I can remember the typeface perfectly—black sans serif from a laser printer—but not the message. I hope it says, "Welcome! You are about to leave the world and enter Charlie's hippie sanctuary. If you work here for a year, it will change you. It may entice you to remain for many years longer, and if you do leave, you'll remember the place forever." But I suspect it says, "Danger! Laboratory Animals! Authorized Personnel Only!"

2

CORRIDOR A

The lab has two corridors. In my mind, the shorter corridor always runs up and down, like the stalk of a stubby capitol T, and the longer corridor runs side to side along the top of the letter. I can't shake that mental model, even though it requires that east point up and north to the left. My hippocampus, the map-making part of my brain, got the space twisted early on and can't untwist itself. The first, shorter corridor, the base of the T, I will call Corridor A, and the longer one I will call Corridor B. You can find them in Figure 1 at the start of this book, which shows the plan of the lab when I walked in at age nineteen and saw it for the first time. Figure 2 shows the state of the lab fifteen years later, modified here and there, when I was thirty-four.

Once you pull open the front door and enter the lab, you'll find yourself looking up Corridor A. It's narrow and low, dimly lit, dominated by a profoundly bizarre beige and blue color scheme. It looks like a prison or a mental hospital.

I walk in, the door closes behind me on its spring, the lock snicks, and I look up to see a massive Colombo flying at me, screaming. Sometimes Mike Colombo plays "scoots," as he calls it. You put on roller blades, unscrew a long wooden broom handle from its broom, and skate up and down the corridors hitting a puck made out of a roll of tape. If you get two or four people playing and designate a goal at either end of the corridor, you can have a lively possibility of a broom handle through the chest. Usually scoots takes place in the longer Corridor B, but this time, I don't know why, Colombo has taken a turn and is barreling down Corridor A. When he hits, by Newton's law, we bounce apart. I crash backward and hit my head on the round glass window of the front door and he falls on his ass. This entertaining medical surprise is possible only because, behind that front door, the space is ours. We don't think of it as part of a public building with a library and classrooms, students and professors. It's our home, and we make up the rules.

As you stand at the start of Corridor A, if you're not confronted by a dramatic flying surprise and have the luxury of looking around, you may notice a silver-colored exit sign above your head, mounted near the entrance door. Normally I ignore it. But if you experience a power-out during the humid summer, when the air conditioners overtax the university's power grid, and the corridor goes black with a chirp of equipment turning off all around you, and you hear the monkeys in the distance squawking in surprise, then the red glowing letters on the exit sign shine out on emergency battery power. As the only light source, the sign dominates the corridor, grinning toothily like a Halloween pumpkin as if it enjoys the malfunction and mischief that has descended on the lab.

Directly to your right stands the door of the lunchroom, usually open. To your left stands the door to the quarantine room. (I recommend you consult Figure 1 and keep it handy.) The two doors and their metal doorframes are painted a psychedelic blue-green, striking against the beige wall paint. That color combination is a fundamental part of the aura of the lab. It is, at the same time, subdued and like a drug trip. Each of these doors has a stainless-steel knob shaped a bit like a wine glass, the foot of the glass attached to the door. There's an aesthetic distinction between the shine of chrome and the shine of stainless steel. Chrome shines harshly like a mirror, whereas stainless steel has a softer reflection with more dispersion. I like the soft dispersion of our doorknobs. The flat forward face of the knob contains a keyhole. On the opposite side of the door, inside the room, the corresponding knob is different. Instead of a keyhole it has a doohickey, a little flat fillip that you can turn to lock or unlock the door.

The lunchroom door has a rectangular grating near the bottom, perhaps two feet wide and a foot and a half tall, painted the same blue-green color as the rest of the door, a set of slats evidently to let air pass freely from the room out to the corridor. Almost all the doors in the lab have this ventilation grille at the bottom, though I have never seen such a thing outside the lab. I think, in our subconscious minds, it connects the lab. We don't have a collection of separate rooms; we have one unified, flowing space. The lab is a whole, a single living cell, its cytoplasm moving freely, and the rooms are its pseudopodia. You can't see through the slats into the room because they're angled the wrong way. But from inside the room, if you look down through the slats, you can catch a glimpse of the floor just outside, enough to see thin fragments of somebody's feet in the corridor.

The door to the quarantine room lacks a ventilation grille. You don't want airflow in and out of quarantine.

The quarantine door, the lunchroom door, all other doors in the lab, are identified by minimalist labels. Each door has a plastic, dark brown, faux-wood plaque, about an inch high and five inches long, with plain white numbers. The plaque is glued on at about head height, stark against the light blue-green of the door. If you run your fingers over the numbers, you'll feel that they're indented into the plastic. Weird little works of pop art, like something from Andy Warhol, the plaques look like they were stamped in a 1960's label machine—which, I presume, they were. I don't remember the number to the lunchroom. Why would I? Imagine putting numbers on the rooms in your house. You know where the kitchen is, where the bathroom is, you don't need to remember them as 1-E-4 or 1-E-5.

Just beyond the doors to the lunchroom and the quarantine room, a yard farther up Corridor A, you see two metal grilles built into the walls, one on either side. They're a tarnished silver color, galvanized steel, made of overlapping horizontal slats that block you from seeing through, and they correspond to the utility spaces indicated in black in Figure 1. They're access hatches to the plumbing and electrical infrastructure. The grilles are about two feet wide and extend from waist height up to just under the ceiling. At some point I hang posters over them. Charlie has mounted two large posters of Vesalius drawings onto foam plastic sheets, and for some mischievous reason, when I'm an undergraduate and have no concept of other people's property, I see the two posters lying on the lunch table, shove paper clips through their upper corners, bend the paper clips into mounting hooks, and hook the posters over the ventilation grilles. Now the corridor has a picture on each side. One is of a walking man, stripped down to his muscles, with an especially obvious muscle fanning out over his left temple. The other is of a skeleton in a graveyard, standing casually with his elbow resting on a marble pedestal, as if he has dug himself up and is contemplating what to do next. They are medieval, black-and-white woodcuts. They greet you like guardians as you walk up the corridor further into the lab. They are silent watchers.

On the left wall of the corridor, just beyond the skeleton who dug himself up, you'll see two large brown corkboards, one after the next, each about four feet wide and three feet tall. They have aluminum frames and are screwed securely to the wall with Phillips head screws. For a long time they're empty, but eventually we pin up some homemade posters leftover from the annual Society for Neuroscience conference. Nobody ever reads the posters—they're wall art, rectangles of colored cardboard with white paper graphs glued to them, the glue coming undone, the paper peeling off, fluttering and rustling quietly as you walk past. Ironically, the posters are on the topic of auditory space—specifically, how neurons in the brain process quiet, rustling sounds within arm's reach of the body.

The opposite wall, the wall to your right, has no corkboards, no posters, just a vast expanse of undecorated, beige cinderblock. In the middle of that expanse, you'll see a dark gray, shiny, cat-sized, metal door, at head height, with a black plastic latch, and if you open it you'll find the fuse box for the lab hidden inside the wall. I won't describe the inside of the fuse box because I've looked in it only a few times. It would not astonish me if someone has hidden a surprise in there, like a plastic mouse or snake.

I want to establish the nature of the floor. It's omnipresent, and if you don't have a picture of the floor then you don't understand the lab. It's made of linoleum square tiles about a foot across, light tan with darker brown flecks that poorly hide the dingy color of age, the hairline cracks between tiles becoming visible from years of impacted dirt. A dark, chocolate brown, linoleum crash-strip, four inches tall, runs along the base of each wall. The crash strip does not perfectly stick to the cement wall, especially where the strip rounds a corner, leaving a tiny space into which dust and dirt can get stuck.

The walls are cinderblocks. When I first arrive in the lab, the light beige color is a little cold, a little brown. The color of stale coffee with a little milk in it. Now that the paint has been redone, the color is warmer, lighter, a hint of peach and yellow sunflower mixed in. The paint is thick, intricately lumpy over the uneven concrete surface of the cinderblocks, and glossy—a waterproof and mold-proof coating. If you put your eye close to it, it looks like a rolling, frozen arctic landscape in the dusk.

The ceiling is tiled in big, off-white slabs made of an unknown crusty substance, like giant pieces of lightly toasted bread, riddled with pores. I hope it's not asbestos because it sheds particles on our heads over time. Metal runners painted white, about half an inch wide, divide the big, two-by-three-foot panels. I know from repair work that the actual ceiling is about four feet higher, an unpainted surface full of squared concrete beams and large diameter pipes. Stiff wires hang down, twist-attached to the metal runners on which the ceiling tiles rest. The ceiling has been hung low. In Corridor A, it's hardly three inches taller than the top of the doorframes. In Corridor B, the ceiling looms even lower, resting directly on top of the doorframes. A peculiar little vertical step in the ceiling, at the end of Corridor A, divides the one height from the other. If you jump up too vigorously, your head will mash into the ceiling tiles and leave a dent.

Corridor A has one fluorescent light fixture, in the angle where the wall and ceiling meet, to your left, directly above one of the corkboards. It shines down on the auditory poster, shedding light on science. The light fixture is about three feet long, covered in a bumpy, translucent, plastic casing. The plastic was probably once white but has gone yellow with age. It's curved outward, fitting into the angle between the wall and the ceiling, a sector of a cylinder, and is held at the ends by tarnished gray metal caps. Because there is only one light, the corridor tends toward dimness. It might seem claustrophobic to you, low and narrow and deprived of natural light, but to me it's as comforting as a home cave.

If you close your eyes and breathe in, you might smell someone's leftover lunch—the pungency of takeout Chinese food scraped into a garbage can in the lunchroom. Or you might smell a very faint zoo odor—a monkey whiff that's everywhere in the lab and waxes and wanes as the colony door opens. Underneath, you'll smell the lab itself—dust, books, paper journals, shedding ceiling tiles, old floor wax, the concrete cinderblocks in the walls. That subtle background smell is not unpleasant, and you won't even notice it unless you pay attention. Whether you're aware of it or not, it constantly tells you that you're here and nowhere else on earth.

3

CORRIDOR B, WEST WALL

Tirin wants a candy bar from the vending machine in the basement. But he's short of pocket money. "Mike," he says, wheeling a green metal chair out of his office and into the middle of Corridor B, "will you give me a dollar if I can jump over my chair?" Tirin is a fixture in the lab like so many of us, a graduate student and then a post doc, year after year, someone who doesn't want to leave.

"Jump without hitting your head?" I say skeptically, glancing at his chair and then up at the low ceiling.

He nods, I nod—certain he'll fail—and he springs over the chair without hesitation or apparent effort. I don't know how. I give him the dollar and he gets his candy bar.

Next time, Charlotte and I challenge him to kick high enough to touch the ceiling with his shoe. He scowls at us, as to say, "What kind of incompetent weakling do you think I am?" He leaps in the air, flings his leg halfway up, and splits his pants. No dollar for the candy machine, and we almost die laughing.

"You know what you looked like?" I say, sputtering with laughter, mocking him, jumping in the air with my arms flapping. It's a karmic moment, I guess. I don't appreciate how little clearance I have between my head and the ceiling, and I don't realize that the ceiling tile directly above my head is special. Most of the tiles are loose and, when hit from beneath, will tilt up into the free space above. But just above this particular tile is a thick insulated pipe holding it down. How could I know? I almost knock myself out. It hurts so much it's sickening. When I recover, I find my unsympathetic friends doubled over, choking in fits of laughter. I've eclipsed Tirin's split pants. That spot in the ceiling of Corridor B has a perfect, round, head-shaped indentation forever.

As you walk up Corridor A, past the two skeletal Vesalius guardians, and Corridor B looms up at you, branching out to either side, first you'll see the back door to Charlie's office directly in front of you. Charlie never uses this particular door— it's blocked up on the inside and therefore isn't really a door so much as a blue part of the wall. You'll see a poster in dark colors tacked to it. As you approach, you might realize that it's Bruegel's famous painting of the blind leading the blind. When asked about it, Charlie shrugs and mutters, with a slight lisp mixed up in his Brooklyn accent, "I gueth thath's the motto of the lab."

We spend a lot of our time in Corridor B. It's the busy central highway of the lab. Some of the décor is the same as in Corridor A. The linoleum floor tiles are the same pale tan, with darker brown speckles, scratched and aged, but still shiny from frequent mopping and waxing. Running along the bottom of the walls is the same dark brown, linoleum crash strip, four inches tall. Near the colony door, a piece of that crash strip keeps falling off because too many monkey cages have been wheeled past and banged against it. We keep sticking it back on with glue, but it never stays. The walls are cinderblock, painted the usual lab beige, interrupted by the many weirdly blue metal doorways and the vast colorful collection of wall art. The corridor is so narrow that I can almost touch both sides with my elbows. Think about that. The ceiling is low, resting on top of the metal doorframes, probably in violation of building codes. In these ways, Corridor B resembles Corridor A. But it has a different feel—a different personality. For one thing, here, you don't get the impression of a cramped space. Mainly, you notice how incredibly long the corridor is—about sixty feet. If it were merely a hallway in a corporate building, sixty feet would be unremarkable, but it's an unusual, stretched shape for the central room of a private house, which is how we understand it.

And the light in Corridor B is different. Because the offices all along the east side have windows, and their doors are usually wide open, shafts of sunlight cut into the corridor, giving it a warmer feel—a living space instead of a bunker. If you stand at one end of the long narrow hallway and look down toward the other end, you'll see a patchy, alternating pattern on the floor of sun-glow and fluorescent lighting.

I've just arrived at the lab, a teenager in love with the inner world of science. No more books and exams; I've discovered the real stuff you can do with your hands. Charlie's lab offers me a mental freedom I don't experience in class or in the library. One of my jobs is to take care of the infant monkeys, and I've made special friends with Barney, taking him out of the monkey room to play with him. Nobody else plays with the monkeys or lets them run free like I do. I think it's against the rules, but me, I'm myopic toward the rules. I see them, but not very well. The regulations are all about numbers on paper, not about caring for the animals with your heart. I want to make a personal connection with the animals and see them happy.

Hillary, the senior post doc in the lab, is sometimes my partner in this heartfelt crime. One of our games is to let Barney run up and down the long, long corridor. To him it must seem an immense distance—he's only the size of a squirrel. He loves the exercise and squeals in delight.

I'm wearing a white lab coat stained with monkey shit, and Hillary is wearing a green surgical gown. Normally, surgical gowns are tied closed in back, but Hillary likes to put them on like a cardigan and tie them in front. I sit on the floor, cross-legged, at the south end of the corridor, just in front of the prep room. Hillary sits on the floor at the north end, in front of the colony. I let Barney go and he gallops down the long hall to Hillary. She catches him, gives him a pet, a scratch behind the ears, lets him go, and he gallops back to me. Sometimes we bowl a whole apple down the hall and he gallops after it, squeaking. If he catches it, he hugs it to his chest with both hands and takes tiny bites out of it, while hopping on his back legs.

At the very end of the corridor, on the door of the prep room, someone has fixed a small corkboard and tacked up a Snellen eye chart. The corridor is so long that only the largest block letters at the top of the chart are legible from the opposite end of the hall. In the middle of the night, when I've been working too long and need a break, sometimes I pitch a tennis ball down the hall and try to nail the chart. At sixty feet, it's almost exactly the distance from a pitcher's mound to home base. Because the hall is narrow and low, however, it's difficult to pitch the distance while maintaining height. It's a challenge, and pretty rare that I succeed. Usually the ball dips below the corkboard and hits the bottom of the door, reverberating against the ventilation grille.

If I succeed and hit the chart, right on the big E, then the door gives a satisfying, resounding thump and a rattle. One night I'm pitching away, muttering to myself, trying to straighten out some thoughts in my head, when suddenly an office door opens nearby and Isaac steps out. He's been sitting in Earl's area the whole time, listening to me talk to myself, and must think I'm crazy. Maybe I am, anyway. I don't know.

I don't think Charlie approves of hall pitching, or of scoots (hockey on roller blades, as I noted before), but he doesn't stop us. He's a tolerant father to the lab. I think he views childish games with a deep skepticism, genuinely puzzled to find any interest or value in them. And yet . . . I don't know who brought in the Rock'em Sock'em Robots game, but Charlie has been known to play it with us. When he does, he grips the levers so hard that cords stand out on his arms, a rage takes over his face, his teeth show in the middle of his bristly wild beard, his whole body jitters, and he slams and jams and bashes the board across the table into your lap and both robots instantly lose their heads. The physical intensity with which he plays is fairly incredible. I don't know if he has the capacity to do anything by half measures.

As Tirin puts it, "It's all fun and games until somebody loses a spleen."

The prep room door, along with the doorframe, entirely caps the end of Corridor B, highlighting how narrow the walls are and how close the ceiling looms. My impression, looking down toward that end of the long corridor, is of colors enclosing colors. Faded blue door, brown corkboard on the door, white eye chart on the corkboard, black letters on the eye chart. Above the corkboard, pasted on the blue front of the door at head height, I can see two brown placards, where almost every other door in the lab has only one. The lower placard contains the room number: 1-E-10. The fact that I remember it is a testament to the importance of the room. The upper, longer placard reads, "No Unauthorized Personnel." The room is one of the sacred spaces in the lab where ancient experiments, long before my time, revolutionized neuroscience. The sign is paranoid, however. Everyone in the lab is authorized, so who is it speaking to? Who is it keeping out? Maybe it dates from before we had a front door, when unwanted neighbors could wander in.

Immediately to the right of the prep room, you turn the corner to the long west wall of the corridor. Think of a long wall in an art gallery. Each picture or installation has a place, a carefully considered position, and between are blank patches of wall painted a neutral beige. Some of the empty patches are wider, some narrower, some of the installations are up near the ceiling and some are closer to the floor, some are as small as a person's hand and some are as large as a refrigerator, in a mysterious arrhythmic pattern that itself holds an aesthetic quality.

First along the wall you'll find the door to the darkroom, later Tirin's experiment room. Another faded, blue, wooden door set in beige cinderblocks, blank except for its neat brown placard and its silvered knob. If you look up, you'll see that just to the right of the darkroom door, tucked directly under the ceiling, a cylindrical stub of plastic tubing sticks out of the wall, jutting beyond the cinderblocks about an inch. It's wide enough that you could slide your arm through, if you stood on a ladder to get up high enough. But if the ladder fell out from under you, you would dangle by your arm and probably break a bone. The tube is painted the same light beige as the wall, and you can even see spots where the paint began to drip down the curving slope of the plastic and then dried in place. I like the idea of a secret opening, a portal from the corridor into the room beyond. It's a cable conduit meant for connecting equipment through the wall, although there aren't any cables passing through it right now and it's blocked up with a mass of black cloth stuffed inside.

To the right of the cable conduit and lower on the wall, a brown corkboard is screwed onto the cinderblocks. It's about four feet wide and three feet tall. Some of our corkboards have a modern aluminum frame—they tend to break apart more easily over time—and some are old-fashioned, with a sturdy wooden frame, and this one is wooden. It has four screws holding it to the wall, two on the top of the frame, two on the bottom, the screw heads slightly raised, slightly tarnished, with a single slot for a flathead screwdriver. For years, one of Tirin's scientific posters on the brain basis of visual attention hangs here. It's on dark blue poster board, which always seems to me a sleepy color for a poster on attention.

In the 1990s, the typical poster is a meticulous arts-and-crafts project. You cut five strips of colored cardboard, each about fifteen inches wide and three feet long, and cover them in graphs and blocks of text on white paper, snipped out with scissors and glued down in a pleasing arrangement. You bring the finished artwork to a conference, present it to a crowd of people, and then bring it home and pin it on the wall. Nobody ever reads the poster again; it's more like a trophy. Tirin's poster has inevitably become tattered, the paper curling off the underlying cardboard, the boards crooked and swinging on their remaining thumbtacks. One of the more peculiar characteristics of an old scientific poster is that, when a thumbtack comes out after a few years, it leaves behind a little circle of vivid, unbleached color where the cardboard surface was protected from sunlight. At the center of the circle is a tiny black puncture mark, like a pupil in an eyeball. Those little blue eyes stare out around the edges of Tirin's poster, watching you as if they're manifesting the visual attention that is the topic of the poster. Since the poster is too big to fit on the corkboard, the final panel is taped to the cinderblock wall with clear, thick packing tape.

To the right of the poster, a few feet away and down at waist height, you'll see an eyewash mounted to the corridor wall. It's a small, silver metal sink, dusty from lack of use. Below the steel basin, a U-bend pipe curves out of the wall, and sticking up above the basin, two faucets are angled to spray into your eyes if you stoop down and push the yellow plastic lever.

As far as I know, the eyewash has only ever been used for two emergencies. The first was a legendary event in the old days, before my time, when Earl walked in on Carl and Carol making out, and ran away with his hands over his eyes screaming, "Eyewash!" I don't think he used the actual eyewash, however.

The second time is when I pour formaldehyde over my head. That's how Charlie describes it, with his penchant for verbal caricature. I don't do it on purpose. The storage room behind the shop (upper right corner of Figure 1) has a high cabinet with old specimen jars. I'm looking through the available brains for a useful one to study, to learn my way around neuroanatomy, and lift down a likely one labeled Earl Gray. Holding the glass jar over a countertop at the back of the storage room, I unscrew the white metal cover and peer inside. The jar is filled with old formaldehyde that has evaporated down to an especially concentrated and odiferous form. A monkey brain about the size of a plum floats inside, and I slosh it around to get a better look at its convolutions. A bit of solution spills over the lip of the jar and the outer glass becomes slippery, especially on my latex exam gloves. The jar slides out of my grip, falls less than a foot, and hits the countertop squarely. With that impact, a tidal wave of formaldehyde shoots up into the air out of the open jar, into my eyes and over my shirtfront.

My first thought is for Earl Gray. I don't want his brain damaged. Did it jump out of the jar along with the fluid? Is it on the floor where I might step on it? I can't manage to open my eyes and see. Then the pain kicks in. I've had no experience with this level of pain. It's beyond comprehension, and I don't know how to respond. Screaming is out of the question— what's the point? I'm silent. At this moment, if someone were to hand me a grapefruit spoon and tell me that scooping my eyes out will fix the pain, I'm sure I'd do it. I come groping out of the storage room blindly, trying to find the eyewash, but my mental map has been destroyed by the pain. I'm stuck in a strange corner bleating, "Hillary? Hillary?"

She must have heard me from her office. I feel her grab onto me and lead me out of the corner. I have just enough extra mental capacity to realize, with embarrassment, that I've been stuck in the shop groping in the tool cabinet, my fingers clunking against screwdrivers. The eyewash, once I reach it and push the handle, pumps out horribly cold water. I can flush my eyes for, at most, a minute before the cold bites at me. Thankfully, the pain subsides and I feel good. I can see again and I think the problem is solved—until, suddenly, I become aware of a fire in my trachea. The fumes must have burnt the lining of my lungs and the pain shoots up into uncharted territory again.

By the time the two paramedics arrive, I'm entirely recovered. My only problem is that I stink of formaldehyde and everyone around me is squinting and coughing. They insist I go with them to the emergency room to have my eyes checked, and they lead me out the back door to the parking lot, where, as I'm being strapped onto their metal gurney and loaded into an ambulance, Julian Jaynes walks past and rubbernecks at me, his bicameral mind visible through his large sad eyes. That's the only interaction I've ever had with the great man.

What I mean is, I have the distinction of being the only person in the thirty-two-year history of Charlie Gross's lab, from the time it was built to the time it was torn down, ever to use the eyewash for a legitimate emergency. Mostly, it's used as a coat hook. You'll often see an old dirty lab coat, a bit tattered, draped over it.

To the right of the eyewash, the histology room door is always open. This room is one of the social centers of the lab, especially during a brain cutting party. It's where the technician spends most of his or her time. Her, I should say, because Charlie always has female technicians. I don't think he's sexist. He's aggressively egalitarian and is especially proud of his many technicians who have advanced to successful academic careers. Maybe he considers the technician job to be a tool for evening out the gender imbalance in science.

If you walk past the histology doorway, a few inches to the right of it you'll find a plastic telephone mounted to the wall of the corridor at shoulder height. It's an intercom for visitors outside the moat—outside the locked, double doors to the east wing. The phone is beige, with five buttons vertically along one side, a long, coiled cord, and a strip of bright pink tape running down the back of the handpiece for no particular reason. If you push button 1, you can talk to the intercom phone outside the lab. If you push buttons 2 through 5, nothing happens. I know; I've tried. I wondered if we could spy in on an intercom in someone else's lab, but no luck.

Next along the gallery wall, to the right of the intercom phone, you'll see a small corkboard only about two feet to a side, a flimsy modern kind with an aluminum border, fixed to the wall at head height. You can already see where the border is beginning to break apart at the corner. The board is a chaos of material: laminated sheets of emergency numbers, vet numbers, protocols, the updated exotic animal license, and a bizarre picture of a glowing blue brain on a black background. Over the years, people add new material, nobody wants to be responsible for removing anything old in case it's somehow important, and therefore a kind of archeological layering has accreted.

If you step just to the right of that bulletin board, you'll find the opening to Corridor A. Darker than Corridor B, a bit more cave-like. Nobody stands around Corridor A chatting. If Corridor B is a long thin living room, or an art gallery, or both, Corridor A is just a corridor. You can look back down toward the Vesalius guardians and the front door of the lab, if you like, or you can step past the dim cave opening to reach the next section of Corridor B, the large stretch of wall beside the surgery room.

This segment of wall is partly decorated with Charlie's beautiful art photos, sky and trees reflected in water, each picture enlarged to about a foot and a half across, mounted neatly on a plastic backing and blue-tacked to the wall. The photos are clustered around a large central whiteboard, which must have been added in the expectation that lab members would stand around in profound scientific debate, drawing equations and brain parts. But the whiteboard is never used for science. The aluminum tray at its bottom is empty—it doesn't even have any dry-erase markers. Instead, Maz, our Iranian graduate student, fills it with a set of magnetic, refrigerator-poetry words. One can buy the innocent version, the suggestive version, or the pornographic version, and we have the suggestive. Over the years, pithy fragments of poetry emerge on that ever-changing forum and I take the trouble of writing down the better ones. It's an ethnographic study. I'm genuinely fascinated by their organic nature, linguistic strangeness, and hint of deeper meaning.

Always cry sausage.

Worshipping together in
My tiny rocking bed.

Please don't want lazy.

Fast car, enormous ship.

Only elaborate beauty could stop me now.

Water is the mother of all drool.

A thousand mean stares from week suited old gowns.

Eat,
Heave,
Beautiful dress.

We urged her to pants him for eternity.

Black honey, purple rust.

Play me a go go symphony.

They're spontaneous koans, each one enigmatic and profound.

I may be fascinated, but Charlie has zero interest in the magnet poetry. When he walks down the hall with his slightly meandering, dyspraxic gate, he'll pass the board without a glance. If you point it out to him, his eye might swivel to it for an instant, he might give his head a dismissive shake, as though privately incredulous at our mental limitations, and then he might say, "How did that data turn out yesterday?" or, "Did you see? That bum Clinton cut Medicaid again!" He's perfectly comfortable grabbing the steering wheel and turning the conversational topic at right angles.

To the right of the whiteboard, near the ceiling, you'll find a metal alarm bell about six inches in diameter, painted thickly in glossy gray. It's connected to a red panic button in the surgery room. If you need help, press the button, and an extraordinarily harsh sound will rip through the lab. Everyone will wonder what calamity has befallen the world, and then, after five or ten seconds of panic, we'll remember that we're supposed to run to the surgery room and help.

The surgery door, just to the right of the emergency bell, is different from the other doors in the lab. It used to be the same type, same blue-green color, same solid wood material, same steel handle I've described before. But a few years after I arrive, the surgery room is renovated. The old one worked beautifully, but we have no choice. The regulators are becoming obstreperous. Around this time, I formulate Graziano's Fundamental Theorem of Regulation: *It only ever gets worse.* That theorem is true. It's a specific manifestation of the second law of thermodynamics.

The new surgery door is painted an approximation to the lab's blue-green color, but less psychedelic, as if the 1960's secret formula has been lost in the meantime. And the texture of the paint is different, slicker, smoother, because the material of the door is different. It's steel. The door is hollow metal instead of

solid wood, and has a large round window filling its upper half.
I suspect the architects saw a surgery door on a TV hospital
show like ER, and gave us what they thought we wanted. But
the window's a disaster. We don't want tourists staring in and
distracting the surgeons. Charlie is so welcoming and warm
a professor that he invites a constant parade of undergrads
into the lab, and we don't want anyone naïve freaking out at
a glimpse of a bloody surgery as they walk down Corridor B.
So we cover the window with a sheet of red plastic cut from
a biohazard bag. As usual for us, something new, something
slick, immediately turns into something makeshift. Someone
with a steady hand does a neat job cutting the material of the
plastic bag into a circle and taping it to the inner surface of the
glass with Scotch tape. On the outside of the circular window,
a white laminated sign has been taped up with transparent
packing tape. It lists all the protective gear that the regulators
tell us we must wear if we enter that room. I used to do brain
surgery without gloves, because the gloves reduce dexterity. I'm
not allowed to anymore.

When you're standing in the hall just outside the surgery
room, if you look down, you'll see some of the surgery floor
peeking out from under the door. The new surgical suite has a
regulation floor. Mudge, Charlie calls it. It's gray and grainy,
apparently made of a mixture of sand and epoxy resin, hard
and waterproof. It's continuous, without tiles or joints, and
extends outward about three inches from underneath the door
before giving way to the old, tan, familiar, linoleum tiles of the
corridor. You can already tell that I'm no fan of the new surgery
suite. It's too professional and perfect, clean and orderly. I'm
most comfortable when immersed in organic, creative chaos.
How can anyone think properly or feel like a human being in a
sterile box of a room?

To the right of the surgery door you'll find a narrow section
of wall, about a foot wide, squeezed between two doorframes.
Beige painted cinderblocks flanked by rising strips of blue-
green metal. That little segment of space plays a special role in
a movie project that stars several lab members and a computer.
The Macintosh computer in my office is a failure—a lemon. I
have to buy a new one, and Tirin, Charlotte, and I devise a plan
for getting rid of the dud. Tirin is the cameraman, holding the
massive black Panasonic VCR camera that we bought to record

some of our experiments. First, we print a sign in black and white, "Effects of lesions to the Nucleus Macintoshus. M. S. A. Graziano, C. S. R. Taylor, T. Moore." The sign is prophetic. The same three authors, in that order, will later appear on a classic paper in cortical physiology. The sign is taped on the wall, framed in that gap between two doorways. The video begins with a tight focus on the sign, then pans out. You see me in a lab coat and bizarre nerd glasses (I don't use glasses), holding the boxy Mac computer tower and heaving it down the hall, toward the colony door. It sails twenty feet in a gentle arc and smashes on the floor tiles. Finally, you see me crouching over it, pulling open the metal casing and calmly smashing its guts to bits with an iron hammer. A cinematic masterwork, and one of the more satisfying moments of my life.

Eventually, Charlie mounts one of his photos on the wall in the same spot where our Nucleus Macintoshus title page once hung. Desert scene, brown sky, black land, hint of a camel rippling in the heat. I wonder if he meant to put it exactly, but exactly, on the same spot. Maybe he's trying to elevate the lab from our puerile sense of fun.

The next door opens onto a geometrically complicated part of the lab. It's not a room, though I think it might have once been intended that way. It's been divided by cheap plasterboard walls into an antechamber that leads into two smaller rooms, little more than closets: the cramped and messy office of Earl the graduate student, and beside it, the room where the baby monkeys live. Later, Earl's office turns into an experiment room, and the antechamber itself becomes an office, crammed full of desks and shelves, used by Tirin and Hillary, then Maz, and eventually Dylan. I think of it mostly as Dylan's office. Dylan lived in the lab as an undergraduate, then as a paid research assistant, then as a graduate student, like so many of us lingering for as many years as he could. The door that faces the corridor is decorated with Dylan's photos, data plots, weird and grotesque pictures cut from magazines, poetry, political stickers, a cardboard cutout of a velociraptor—a flapping clutter as you walk past down the hall.

We have a rubber hand in the lab that looks plausibly real until you inspect it closely and discover how pitted and grubby it is. It's used as a visual stimulus—a few regions in the brain are known to process the sight of hands and other body parts—

but it has a range of other, less scientific functions as well. For example, to the right of Dylan's door, high up on the corridor wall, just under the ceiling, you'll see another cable conduit—a bit of plastic pipe sticking out of the wall—and we insert the hand such that the fingers dangle out over your head as you walk past. Dylan doesn't say a word. It certainly doesn't startle him. His wheelhouse of humor is bizarre enough that a hand emerging from the wall hardly rates.

The fire inspector visits. I'm surprised we can pass any kind of inspection because the lab is one gigantic hazard, a rat's nest of wires and flammable clutter, but somehow the inspector approves every part of the lab except the dangling hand. These regulation guys, they have no sense of humor. The sour, long-suffering look on his face says, "Aaand, that's the *fifth* hand-in-the-wall I've seen since Monday. Great."

Out loud, he says, "You have to lose the hand."

"Why?" we say, indignantly.

He's patient, holding his frustration under control, his eyelids half closed. "If there's a fire and a lot of smoke, someone might think it's a person and try to rescue it. You're putting a fireman's life at risk for a joke."

I hate it when the rules are reasonable; you can't fight against them. The hand goes back in the stimulus drawer until the next comic inspiration.

The stretch of corridor wall to the right of Dylan's room is vast, about fourteen feet wide. It's partly covered by two large corkboards side by side, the old-fashioned kind with wooden frames, scientific posters tacked to them. The posters change over the years, but two in particular survive until the end of the lab. The first poster, one of Tirin's, is mounted on strips of dark blue poster board, his color of preference, and to the right of it, the second poster, one of my own, is mounted on bright orange board, my color of choice. Both are tattered, the printed graphs and blocks of text loose and curling off. One panel is badly gashed from a game of scoots, or maybe from the sharp corner of a monkey cage wheeled past on its way to the cage wash.

Tirin and I are playing a game. We've taken six dry-erase markers and stuck them together, end to cap, in a single long colorful rod about two feet tall, and we're competing to see who can balance the rod on one palm. Tirin tries, I try, I don't remember which one of us loses control, but the marker rod breaks apart and an uncapped blue marker flies through the air and leaves an ugly streak across the face of my poster, which, ironically, is on the topic of neurons in the cerebral cortex that fire up when something flies unexpectedly into your face. It bothers me that this dumb game ruined my poster and not Tirin's, even though the poster is pretty much in tatters anyway. But as tattered and streaked as my poster may be, nothing will ever knock it down, I tell you, because I didn't pin it to the cork with thumb tacks. I nailed it to the solid wooden frame around the edge of the corkboard. I took a hammer, I took some half-inch nails, and I nailed it down permanently. Take that, entropy. A part of me is secretly pleased because my scientific poster is better than Tirin's, at least in the matter of durability.

To the right of the orange poster, the final few feet of the wall are blank, beige painted cinderblock, and then you reach a corner. That corner has little chunks knocked out of the cinderblocks, the grainy and crumbly cement exposed underneath the shiny layer of paint. Too many heavy supplies have been maneuvered around the corner in bulky carts. Sometimes I think I can smell the musty odor of concrete near that end of the corridor, but I may be smelling an unclean fug from the back hall, and anyway, the smell of monkey shit and cleaning solvent tends to mask everything at that end of the lab.

If you turn the corner, you face a short segment of corridor that leads to the back door. You could call it Corridor C, I suppose, but it's really a right-angle bend in Corridor B. That segment, or stub, is badly lit—it has no light fixture of its own, only a reddish tint from the glowing exit sign. Nothing decorates the walls except black streaks and scratches from supply carts wheeled through. There is no reason to hang art here because nobody would look at it. We're in too much of a hurry passing in and out of the lab to pay attention. On the way out, we're hungry for lunch or dinner, sleep or a date. On the way in, we're hungry for data. Maybe you could think of that dim, dirty stub of a corridor as an art installation of its own.

The back door, in shadow in the recess of that stub of corridor, looks like the standard blue wooden lab design, scuffed and streaked from passing carts, but instead of a round steel doorknob, it has a steel crash bar. If you push it, the door swings outward toward your left. A spring automatically closes it behind you. The screws on the crash bar are coming loose; consequently the mechanism rattles and jiggles as you push. It's like a welcome bell in a shop. We all know that distinctive thump and rattle of someone passing through the back door. Every house has distinctive sounds that tell you where people are and what they're doing, like a sonogram. Occasionally I've taken a screwdriver from the shop to tighten the screws, but they always come loose in a few days anyway. Once, one of the screws fell out, was lost, and somebody scrounged up a replacement from the shop. Now the screw on one side of the crash bar doesn't match the screw on the other side.

If you go out the door you'll find yourself in the back hall, an oddly shaped bit of waste architectural space between the lab and the Psychology library. You can look through our lab midden, the pile of old discarded equipment, or you can visit the small restroom if you need to. You can also exit the building, cross the street, and buy lunch at Cox's deli. When you return with your lunch and key yourself in through the back door of the lab, you'll find yourself in Corridor B once again, standing next to the door to the colony. The colony is the all-important room where the monkeys live.

Just to the left of the colony door, hanging under the ceiling and strategically positioned to be visible along the entire length of Corridor B, you'll find the red glowing exit sign. It is mendacious. If you don't know the layout of the lab, you'll naturally assume that the monkey room door is the indicated exit, in which case you're going to die in a fire emergency. Look and see for yourself how far the colony door is from the actual exit, the back door.

Dropping vertically from the exit sign, a beige-painted metal pipe about half an inch in diameter runs down the wall to an alarm box at elbow height. The box is made of tarnished silvery metal, probably aluminum, about three inches tall, about two inches wide and deep, fixed to the wall just to the left of the colony door. A little bit of white, gritty, cement dust always seems to be scattered on the top surface of the alarm box, maybe having crumbled from the cinderblocks behind it when the box was first installed with screws. The alarm must siphon electrical power from the exit sign, hence the pipe connecting the two. I think the concept is that, if the power goes out, which happens frequently, then whatever emergency power is supplying the glowing exit sign will also keep the alarm operational. Each of us has a little silver alarm key like a talisman. Put your alarm key in the slot in the forward face of the box, turn the key from the horizontal to the vertical position, and the alarm is set. If you push the colony door open, you'll jump at a loud crashing buzz and reflexively yank the door closed again to turn off the dreadful racket. Campus security will also receive the signal, and by and by, someone in a security uniform might come knocking. Or might not. They're casual. Someone has helpfully drawn directly on the silvered face of the box with a black marker, "ON" and "OFF" just in case you forget which position is which. During the day, the alarm is always off, and at night, usually someone remembers to turn it back on before leaving. If our attempts at security seem a peculiar combination of elaborate and casually forgetful, note that in the thirty-two years that the lab existed, nobody ever tried to break into the monkey colony. Never.

Except once.

4

CORRIDOR B, NORTH END

To explain the break-in, I'll start by describing the door. The colony door is made of the same sturdy, blue-painted wood as any other doors in the lab, except that it lacks a ventilation grille at the bottom—it's solid for extra security. It has a regular steel doorknob, but also an extra dead bolt about a foot above the doorknob. We have two locks *and* an alarm key. The door has a small, rectangular window about the size of a normal sheet of paper, at head height. For a long time, the window is clear glass, and we can peer in and watch the monkeys chillaxing in their home cages. Eventually, someone covers the glass on the inside with a piece of tan-gray cardboard from the back of a pad of paper. The cardboard fits perfectly into the window—it's exactly the right size and shape.

One day, the door sticks and Tirin can't get out of the colony. Maybe the lock is broken, maybe the wood swelled up in the humid air, maybe a monkey cage, wheeled out of the colony, hit the edge of the doorway and bent the frame by an invisible millimeter. Whatever the reason, the door is stuck. At first, we don't even notice Tirin banging on the inside. We're used to the banging and clanging, hooting and grunting, as monkeys interact, so it takes us a while to realize that a human is adding to the racket. Tirin has peeled the cardboard off the window so he can look out and wave to us. We can hear his muffled voice through the door, but nothing we do on the outside helps.

Hugo, the animal caretaker, strides up. He's ready to clean the monkey cages and sweep the floor, but he can't get in any more than Tirin can get out. Hugo is a priceless human being and a fixture in the lab for two decades. He's a small, muscly man with short white hair, an unconscious John Wayne swagger as he walks, a thick Mexican accent, and a calm, mild, sometimes sardonic, and always laconic way of speaking. Seeing that the door is hopelessly stuck and Tirin is trapped, Hugo shrugs and mutters, "He be okay. There enough monkey biscuits for he to live." Then he walks away.

Eventually, campus security arrives, two meaty men in uniform who take charge. "Stand back," one man shouts impressively, taking a running start at the door and bouncing off by the shoulder. He looks like he's in acute clavicle pain and the door has not even vibrated. The second officer unleashes a karate kick and, by the look on his face, may have shattered a bone in his leg. I'm developing respect for the strength of our door.

Finally the machinist, Jim Watson, a mechanically gifted genius and one of our favorite people in the building, hears about the problem and arrives with his tools. A bit of drilling, a good hour of work on the hinges, and finally the door comes off and Tirin is freed. The point is, the only time anyone ever tried to break into the monkey colony in thirty-two years, it was us, and it took five hours and every emergency department in the university to get through.

The glass in that little square window is eventually replaced by a steel plate for added security. Someone has a bright idea and puts a phone in the monkey room, mounted on the wall next to the door, so you can call out in case of emergency. Discussing these developments among ourselves, we speculate about which monkey is most likely to escape his home cage, reach the phone, and call the outside world, and who exactly he'd call. My bet is on The Mole calling his stockbroker and asking for more biscuit shares. "Rrr. Ah. Rrr. Biscuits."

Like the prep room door facing it at the opposite end of the long corridor, the colony door has two brown placards, one that gives the room number (1-E-16) and the other that gives a warning ("No Unauthorized Personnel"). I will always remember the room number of the colony because the title page of my graduate thesis, in mockery of the university's rules, says, "A thesis presented to the Monkeys of 1-E-16." The colony door also contains a variety of signs taped up here and there with lists of rules and required protective gear. Breathing mask, head bonnet, eyewear, lab coat, exam gloves, paper shoe covers. Absolutely no entrance without complete Personal Protective Equipment. They don't even call it by its full name anymore. They call it PPE. When you see obscure initials replacing ordinary English words, you know you're dealing with an officious mentality. Regulatory creep; that's what it is. By "creep," I mean, "Those regulators are creeps."

Once, in the middle of the night when no one else is around, I walk into the colony room barefoot and naked, just to see how the monkeys will react, but they don't care. They're unimpressed by my anatomy. They don't show any curiosity about our species differences. They may be too sleepy, or too grumpy about the sudden light waking them up, or they may have no interest in what us humans look like under our clothes. I'm disappointed. Still, the experiment yielded data, and you must accept your data for what it is.

The colony floor is raised about six inches above the floor of the hallway. The doorway, consequently, incorporates a step. We used to lift cages and carts up that inconvenient step to get them across the threshold and into the colony. Now Jim the shop guy has made us an elegant steel ramp with black traction treads. It extends outward about two feet in front of the colony door, slanting down to the linoleum tiles of the corridor, and collects grime and monkey hair around the edges because of the janitor's understandable difficulty fitting a mop or broom into the tight spaces.

Our lab technician, Nancy, is wheeling an empty monkey chair out of the colony, down the ramp. The chair is made of Lexan (a strong, transparent plastic), and is resting on a cart made of aluminum rails with black hard plastic wheels that swivel all directions. The whole assemblage is probably about four feet tall and thirty pounds. It runs away from her and tips down the ramp, crashing over. To save the chair from sliding off its cart and breaking on the floor, she reaches out to grab it, but her right index finger is caught and squeezed between two falling pieces.

The rest of us are eating in the lunchroom, far away and around a corner, when we hear the scream. I dismiss it as the sound of an enthusiastic conversation, but Charlie is more attuned. His people radar is uncanny. He rushes out of the lunchroom, hair quivering, feet shuffling in Birkenstocks, to find Nancy in excruciating pain, weeping. He leads her to the sink in the surgery room where she can run cold water on her finger. A few minutes later I look in to ask if she's okay, and I see her still trembling, with tears leaking out, her hand under the faucet and her foot on the cold-water pedal. "No," she says, "not really, but I will be. I think I just have to suck it up in the meantime, Mike." This moment is the first time I ever hear the phrase, "suck it up," used in the wild. It's just coming into vogue at the time, in the 90s.

Meanwhile, Charlie is shuffling around the lab trying to find ice for Nancy's finger, but we don't have any. The best he can dig up is a frozen chunk of pig from the most recent animal roast party, stored in the lab freezer. For the rest of the day, Nancy walks around the lab cradling an enormous pig haunch wrapped up in a green surgical towel.

The lab, in some ways, reminds me of a brain. Long ago, in the 1920s, the Canadian neurosurgeon Wilder Penfield began a series of remarkable experiments. When tasked with removing a brain tumor from a patient, he'd open up the patient's head under local anesthetic, expose the surface of the brain, and then electrically stimulate using a metal stylus to deliver a mild current. The idea was to map out different parts of the cerebral cortex, so that when he removed brain tissue, he wouldn't take out someone's speech area. Stimulate here, and the arm twitches. Stimulate there, and the person claims to see a flash of light. In the temporal lobe, stimulation evoked memories so vivid that the patients sometimes thought the imagery was real. One woman thought actual music was playing. As soon as the stylus was lifted from the surface of her brain, and therefore the electrical current was interrupted, the music shut off.

The inside of the lab is like a living brain, the walls like the convoluted surface of the cerebral cortex. Every locus I touch, no matter how small, has a universe of thought and emotion attached to it and stories spooling out of it. So we move around the lab, touching one spot after the next with the electrified stylus.

5

CORRIDOR B, EAST WALL

We're ready to turn the corner from the door of the monkey room and explore the long, east wall of Corridor B. A segment of cinderblock wall, about five feet long, separates the colony door from my office door. I don't think that kind of proximity would be legal anymore. Too much fear of germs, disease, dirt and chaos. But in those days, we lived cheek-by-fuzzy-jowl with the monkeys.

At the top of this segment of wall, running under the ceiling, you'll find the first of the four fluorescent light fixtures in the corridor. A curved segment of translucent plastic, a sector of a cylinder about a yard long and eight inches wide, fits into the angle between the wall and the ceiling. The plastic is bumpy, textured, slightly yellowed, and cracked. Probably somebody hit it with a broom handle while playing scoots. It's capped by aluminum end plates. The fluorescent lights are extremely bright and even at night give the impression of daytime in the lab, although they lack the warmth of real sunlight.

Everything that Jim, the shop guy, built for us, has an aura now. After he died of spinal cancer, a bit of his fundamentally kind and conscientious personality clings to his handiwork around the lab. About a foot under the light, at eye level, you'll see a convenient shelf that he made for us out of varnished, blond wood. It's about six inches deep, extends across the five-foot segment of wall, and contains a bouquet of protective equipment for anyone about to enter the colony: colorful boxes of latex gloves, boxes of white paper bonnets and blue paper shoe covers, boxes of white and pink facemasks with tan elastic bands. Because you have to look up to reach the supplies, and the shelf is directly under the long bright light, getting shoe covers or protective gloves has become a specific aesthetic experience, intense, illuminating, squint-inducing, like a sudden religious realization. I doubt Jim thought he would leave behind a shrine of PPE under a fluorescent light as a remembrance of himself, but I think he would have enjoyed it.

Just under the shelf, you'll see a plank, also made of varnished, blond wood, screwed flat to the wall, with a row of eight brass hooks sticking out. The hooks hold plastic face shields dangling by their straps, a few green plastic goggles, and about a dozen lab coats. The lab coats are white, or off-white, where the "off" part is old monkey shit. In later years, we also have purple plastic jumpsuits that close with metal snaps to keep the shit off when you clean the colony. On the floor beneath the mass of coats you'll often find a gaggle of old warped shoes, mainly worn-out sneakers and rubber boots—colony footwear that people have brought in for themselves. On weekends and vacations, the graduate students clean the colony. I've done it myself many times. You put on full protective gear, slide into the translucent-purple plastic jumpsuit, put on a large plastic face shield with a gray strap around your head, and lumber into the colony room like a beekeeper to hose and sweep and squeegee the place. Then you come out drenched in sweat and peel off the layers. Honestly, I prefer going in with my regular clothes, maybe a cotton lab coat buttoned over the top, a large flapping one that leaves me plenty of air circulation, so I'll sweat less. On Christmas, if nobody else is around, Charlie cleans the colony. He says it's fun—hosing shit is like playing with mud pies.

To the right of that supply shelf stands the door to my office, usually open, with a whisper of subdued sunlight filtering into the corridor. I always have my shade pulled because I don't like direct sunlight. I'm part vampire, evidently. It used to be Paul's office. Or Hillary's. Or Colombo's. Or Tom's. People do tend to shuffle around. Now that it's all mine, I've taped a poster to the outside of the door, a beautiful charcoal drawing that a friend of Dylan's made for the lab. Think of Da Vinci's Vitruvian man, the one with four arms and four legs inscribed in a circle. The drawing I have on my door shows a macaque monkey in the same pose, complete with backward Leonardo writing.

Next along the corridor, to the right of my office door, is a segment of wall about two feet wide with a single screw stuck into it at shoulder height. Screws are usually fixed into concrete in a specific manner. You drill a hole in the concrete, hammer in a plastic insert, and then twist the screw into the insert. Here, the insert is red. You can just see the rim of it around the shaft of the screw. Sometimes nothing is hanging from the screw—it's just sticking out of the middle of the beige-painted cinderblock, in itself an aesthetic comment. If, in the middle of a casual conversation in the hallway, you lean back against the wall, that screw will dig painfully into your spine between the shoulder blades and possibly rip a hole in your green T-shirt that you just bought. After a while, Charlie uses it to hang one of his landscape photos in a white frame with a glass front. The frame just fits, side to side, in that narrow strip of wall.

To the right of the framed photo stands the door to the secretary's office. For a while, Hank is our secretary. He's an evangelical Christian who must relish the challenge of working in a lab of heathen scientists. He talks to Xintian about God. Xintian is too polite to tell him to fuck off. Then he tries Shalani, a Christian with a deep belief of her own, who is also too polite to tell him that he's an offensive creep. Then he tries Maz.

"Have you ever thought about Jesus, Maz?"

"Don't waste your time on me, Dude," Maz says. "I'm Muslim."

That shuts him up.

Charlie fires him when he finds out about the gay bashing. Turns out, Hank's passion project is a pray-the-gay-away reform program that he's trying to institute on campus.

The next secretary is an antidote. Tyler is one of our best secretaries and a long-time friend of the lab. He's an ex-Mormon opera singer, an enormous guy with a booming voice, a huge smile, and a balding blond head. He sings for the New York Metropolitan Opera and works for us during the day. Partway through his time with us, he comes out as gay, telling each of us privately because he wants the people he works with to know and understand. He sits down in my office in the big, uncomfortable, but impressive wooden throne that I've put in there recently for guests, and earnestly explains that he has something to tell me that might affect our working relationship, but he hopes that it won't. Then he blurts it out. I don't react the best way. I wish I could do it over. I'm sure I look surprised and slightly frightened at hearing about someone else's private life. I put out my hands as if I'm trying to protect myself from a hose, a reflexive gesture, and say, "That's totally your business and

up to you, and definitely won't affect how we work together."
It does, of course. It takes down some barriers and makes us
more comfortable with each other. But I wish I had reacted like
Charlie, who, apparently, when told, lit up with a huge smile
and congratulated Tyler on a courageous moment in his life.

We've had many other secretaries in that little room—Shari,
Andrea, Monica—but Maida was its longest-running occupant,
and when I think of that space, she's sitting in it, shouting back
and forth to Charlie about how to format a document, both
of them with voices as loud as honking geese and with thick
Jewish Brooklyn accents.

On the door of Maida's office, someone has thumbtacked
a poster, a detailed and realistic ink drawing of a baboon on a
leash. The baboon is sitting on its haunches, looking casually to
its right, one hand resting down against its genitals apparently
in an attempt to fig-leaf the naughty part. But rather than
preserving the innocence of the piece, the posture rather looks
like the baboon is masturbating.

Anytime you want to talk to Charlie, you stick your head in
Maida's office (the door is always open) and look through an
inner door to see if he's at his desk. Maida works for us only
three hours a day, three days a week, and the rest of the time
her space functions as the vestibule to Charlie's office. It also
contains the shared printer and therefore acts like a watering
hole on the Serengeti. Sooner or later, we each must make our
daily visit. I think Charlie likes that sociable arrangement where
everyone in the lab passes through his vestibule. It must give
him a daily census. Sometimes, as you walk down the hall, you
hear his voice rising up like a mid-register bassoon, "Hello?
Hello? Maida? Maida? Michael? Tirin?" as if he's engaging in
a kind of sonar test for people, checking what bounces back.
Sometimes we come in to say hello, or sit and gossip, or talk
science. Sometimes we're too preoccupied, perhaps wheeling
a monkey past to perform his daily button-pressing job.
Sometimes we can hear Charlie's scratchy old radio tuned to
the classical station.

To the right of Maida's door, on the next segment of the
corridor wall, a corkboard is pinned with chaotic, overlapping
layers on layers of postcards and snapshots. A picture of a
Maori with a heavily tattooed face. A picture of Charlie in a
vivid blue and orange tie-dye T-shirt, running with his arms up

in the air through the finish line at the New York Marathon, with a time of just over five hours lit up in orange lights over his head. Not a bad time, by the way. A bizarre picture that Tirin and Paul made of my hairy, bearded head grafted onto the body of a female bikini model. A largely unused chalkboard is fixed to the wall next to the corkboard. The aluminum tray has a few broken pieces of chalk, a great deal of dust, a couple post cards propped up, often an open soda can that somebody set down in the middle of a conversation and then forgot. The chalkboard has a weird iridescence, a sheen, partly from old chalk dust that solidified in the New Jersey humidity, and partly from the glare of a fluorescent light fixture running directly above it.

The famous Ricardo poster hangs further down the wall. It catches your eye as the most prominent, bizarre, and austere object in the corridor. The poster is an ancient, legendary, half-ruined work of art from the twelfth century BCE, or from 1970, whichever is earlier—I'm not sure. It's wedged into the four-foot space between a painted, vertical pipe stretching down the wall and the blue metal edge of a doorway. It's no poster-board trifle—it's a massive construction, extending from about knee height to ceiling height, made of thick, white-painted wood and securely mounted to the wall with silvery screws all around its edge. The text for the poster looks like it was typed on a manual typewriter, cut out with scissors into little uneven rectangles, and glued on here and there, although the glue has gone brown and crusty with age and is visible through the paper in X marks and squiggles. The display showcases beautiful models of brain areas made out of real copper wire frames. The idea was that an area of the cerebral cortex might be naturally curled up in a complex way, but if it could be duplicated in a copper frame that is hand-welded together, the frame could then be straightened with pliers, revealing what the brain area might look like structurally if it were spread flat on a table—like flattening the ball of the globe onto a map. Now-a-days, a computer can manipulate a virtual model, but apparently in the decades before my time in the lab, real wire models were the cutting edge of science. The poster reminds me of the physical models of DNA that were *de rigueur* in the 1960s. The copper wire models are fixed to the poster with silver wire twist-ties. The front of the poster is covered with a sheet of clear plastic material, like food wrap, which, over time, shreds and dangles in ragged strips. It looks like dripping ectoplasm. The sharp edges of the copper models often snag on our lab coats as we walk past. This ruinous, monumental art collage, beautiful and outdated, enigmatic after most of its parts and labels fall off, remains in the lab screwed to the wall, decade after decade, a testament to the endurance of science and the passage of time, until the very end when the wrecking crew comes and turns the lab to rubble.

What I mean, I think, is that anything and everything in the lab, whether it's meant to be a visual display or is just a pipe or a telephone or a scratch in the paint, eventually turns into a comment on life and experience and ambition and endurance and evanescence and endings and death.

Take, for example, the Bruegel painting. To the right of the Ricardo poster stands the back door to Charlie's office. As I already explained, he never uses this door. It's blocked by a table on the inside of the office. Its only purpose in the lab is to serve as a blue backdrop, essentially a large wooden frame, for a poster of Bruegel's *The Blind Leading the Blind*. This dark-toned painting shows six blind peasants trying, unsuccessfully, to lead each other by a series of hand-held sticks. The front peasant, with a look of dismay, has just fallen into a ditch. The poster is tacked up with four silver tacks, one in each corner, driven into the wood of the door.

I think Charlie is right—the painting captures the essence of science, which is harder than anyone, especially scientists, typically realize. You stumble around, you encounter sudden and disconnected details as if encountering twigs and pebbles with your blindly groping fingers, you publish proud papers on those trivial details, you expend a lifetime of effort, but how many genuine scientific discoveries do you ever really make when you can't see far? Very few. Some scientists, some with the most successful careers and inflated egos, would not know a genuine insight if they fell head-first into it like the stumbling peasants in Bruegel's painting.

To the right of the Bruegel door stands a stretch of wall, perhaps five feet wide, shining brightly under a light fixture. When I first arrive, this spread of wall contains one enormous whiteboard on which the monthly calendar is kept—a grid of days drawn in black marker, the squares relabeled each month. We schedule surgeries, experiments, pig roasts, visiting scholars, conferences, people's individual vacations.

In my early days, Charlie is meticulous about the daily schedule and he participates in every lab event. He has a touch of the obsessive compulsive in him, maybe as compensation for the chaos inherent in his personality. Later, that immense whiteboard wears out, develops wrinkles and cracks, and is taken off the wall. Charlie insists that we replace it with a new one, claiming that you can't run a lab without a proper schedule board. Unfortunately, his impulse for organization comes up against his instinct for financial frugality. Giant whiteboards have become absurdly expensive. The replacement, therefore, is a much smaller board that doesn't suit the monthly schedule. With some skeptical, disappointed grunts from Charlie, a part of the lab tradition dies. We never much use the new white board and Charlie becomes just that much less connected to the events in the lab. The experiments are no longer centrally organized—we're more like a collection of separate minilabs run by the postdocs and graduate students.

Eventually, to either side of the small, new white board, Charlie mounts several more of his photos, three to the left side, two to the right. They're wilderness sunset pictures. Charlie is focusing less on his science, more on his art, and somehow in doing so he makes the rest of us feel empowered, as though he's handing off a legacy and letting us become the custodians of science in the lab.

To the right of this cluster of photos stands the door to another office. Hillary's and Seamus's, Mike Colombo's, Paul Azzopardi's, Tirin's, Hillary's when she returns, Tirin's when *he* returns. Members of Charlie's lab have a habit of moving on and then coming back to the sanctuary a few years later, when the cold outside world overwhelms them. Bungee students, you could call them. Nobody fits that pattern better than me—I went to MIT for two years and then came back forever.

One quirk of this office door is worth noting. Toward the top of the metal door frame, on the inward-facing surfaces, you will find a pattern of drill holes. Mike Colombo put them in, mounting a heavy steel shower rod. It looks like a chin-up bar but is much too high—you'll bash your head on the lintel if you try to use it that way. Along with the bar, Mike bought a set of boots with metal hooks at the heels. If you securely lace on the boots and put the hooks over the metal bar, you can hang upside down like a bat. The device comes with the claim that, by reversing the polarity of gravity on your body an hour a day, you can reverse the process of aging. Colombo, the humorist, cannot resist the purchase. We've all tried it many times, and I find it more comfortable than you might expect. I can hang casually in the doorway for minutes on end, like a giant fruit bat, my arms crossed over my chest to stop my T-shirt from sliding and exposing too much of my stomach. But creeping worries about blood pooling and maybe causing capillaries to burst eventually sour us on it, and Colombo takes down the bar. If you look closely, you'll see two sets of drill holes, indicating where he mounted the bar, realized it was too low (his head bonked on the floor), and then re-mounted it higher up.

A metal pipe runs down from the ceiling, just to the right of Colombo's office. The pipe is about an inch thick and emerges from a small hole cut neatly in the ceiling tiles. It extends down the wall, held in place by metal brackets screwed into the underlying cinderblocks, the metal painted thickly in the same glossy beige as the wall, and ends in an electrical outlet box about shin height off the floor. All the electrical wiring in the lab is strung through pipes that run over the surface of the walls in primitive geometric patterns. Metal and concrete, painted metal and painted concrete, that's the background texture of the lab. The walls are crawling with pipes, some obvious in their functionality and some mysterious. Some pass straight down, some make right angle bends, some disappear through little mouse-sized holes in the concrete, some end in electrical outlets or light switch boxes.

Next to the pipe, Mike Colombo hangs a display item on the corridor wall—a beautiful old, carven, wooden picture frame. He found it in the shop, and a creative idea sprang into his head. The frame has no picture, and you can look through it to the cinderblock wall behind. With a black marker, Colombo reaches through the lower right corner of the frame and signs the wall. It's *avant garde* art, you see. Ultimate minimalism. Maybe it's a sarcastic comment on modern art— there's nothing to see. Or maybe it's exactly the opposite—the epiphany that art is not what's in the frame, but everything that gives it context: the wall, the lab, the world. Or maybe it's just a dumb joke.

Eventually, Colombo's signed-wall installation is replaced by two of Charlie's landscape photos.

Next along the corridor wall, you'll see the fourth, final fluorescent light shining down on another corkboard. Over the years, this space becomes what we call the crazy board. I respect people who know nothing about neuroscience and ask honest questions, but sometimes an idiot will fake a show of knowledge. One letter is a homophobic screed. Another is a salad of random famous equations and terminology, stuck together with no thread or sense, more disturbing than amusing. A third illuminates us with its wisdom: "In my newest theory, which you would do well to adopt, people do not actually have brains. Instead, we *use* brains." This last one is delicious in every ridiculous and arrogant turn of phrase, even more so when we find out that it's a fake crazy message perpetrated by Dylan and secretly mailed to the lab.

Immediately to the right of the crazy board, past the switch that controls the lights in Corridor B, stands the door to the shop room. Almost every door, as I have said, has a grille at its bottom, allowing free airflow from room to hallway. The shop has a peculiarity—its grille is put on upside down. I'm pretty sure the grille is supposed to be oriented for privacy such that you can never see inside a room, but this one has been flipped by mistake. If the door is closed and you stand in the hall looking down through the overlapping blue slats, you can just make out a bit of the floor inside the shop. I like small, secret anomalies that add to the richness and character of a place.

To the right of the shop, the wall turns a corner in its last few inches and touches the prep room door.

Now we've come full circle around Corridor B and looked at every part of it, sixty feet up and sixty feet back down the other way. In the process, I've discovered something I didn't expect. I honestly thought I'd be able to describe every detail I can remember. That turns out to be impossible. I'm realizing now just how much information a brain can contain, quietly tucked away, because my account would be at least a hundred times longer if I truly downloaded the contents of my memory. I remember particular marks on the wall, and the exact pattern of flanges on the ventilation grilles in the ceiling, and each specific light switch and electrical outlet, and where the wall-paint was put on inexpertly and dried while dripping, and a colorful citizenship brochure hanging by a bit of string from a pipe on the wall, and the cardboard inspection tag dangling from the eye-wash, and the inch-wide brown strips on the linoleum floor that divide the inside of each room from the corridor, and the shape and color and wear pattern on the part of each doorway where the bolt slides when the door is closed, and the beige plastic trash can next to the colony door with the white paper sign taped to it that says, "Medical Waste," in hand-written lettering, but nobody can read it because it's been bleached by years of light exposure, and the exact way that one poster on the wall is folded and another one is dog-eared, and a particular wire looping from the ceiling, and the sound of the colony door closing, and the time we were trying to ride Tirin's dirt bike up and down the corridor and left streaks on the floor, and the time Charlie sat in a green metal chair, one of the old rattling kinds, and rolled it with his feet out of his office, down the corridor to Dylan's area, and joined an experiment, without bothering to get up out of the chair, because his back hurt. I can't write it all down. I'm sorry to discover that I can't. It would take me longer to write it than it did to live it, maybe.

6

THE LUNCHROOM

It's time to leave the corridors and visit the rooms behind the doors. Since the lunchroom is inviting and smells like food, it's a good place to start. When you enter the lab through the front door, it's the first room you see, wide open on your right, lively, probably a whole group of people sitting around the table talking loudly.

I've only just started to work in the lab. I'm an undergraduate, skinny, somewhat excessively hairy around the face, with weird, dark brown, intense eyes peering out of the tangles. I know there's a birthday party for somebody, beats me who, I don't yet have a fix on the lab members. I arrive late to the party from my class beforehand, letting myself in with the key I've only recently been given, feeling secretly pleased and important because of that key.

Everyone is standing around the lunchroom, their plates and forks clumped with the remains of white icing. The plates are cheap white ceramic with a blue willow pattern. The cake box on the table is empty except for a few wet bits of icing. I don't mind. I really don't. But Charlie takes it personally, booming in his Brooklyn accent, "He came for the party and we ate all the cake! We can't let that happen! Michael! Michael! Here!" He shoves a plate in my hand and starts to scrape the dregs from his own plate and other people's onto mine, which is frankly disgusting. But the impulse is so generous and lovely that I can't refuse. I nibble at the secondhand mush, feeling slightly ill about contamination, but I admit the icing is pretty good. How can you resist someone so warm and engaging?

When you step into the lunchroom and look around, your first impression is that you've left the dim, cave tunnel of Corridor A and entered an open, lit chamber, where you can breathe more easily. The ceiling of the lunchroom, as for all the lab's rooms, reaches up a good two feet taller than in the corridor. If you jumped, your head would be in no danger of crashing into the tiles. The room has two large, rectangular, fluorescent light fixtures in the middle of the ceiling and is starkly bright when the lights are on, pitch black when the lights are off. There is no natural light in this part of the lab, no windows in the lunchroom or in the entire west end—it's all bunker. It's a private place for us, sequestered from the outside world.

Directly to the right, as you look in the door of the room, you'll see a large refrigerator, a point of convergence for the lab. You can just see how grimy the floor has become beneath it, where the janitor can't reach with his mop. The old Gross lab refrigerator is a white, boxy, 1960's model with rounded corners. It has an actual latch handle, a chrome handle that you tilt upward to open the door. Fridges with latches are illegal so that children don't trap themselves inside, but we have an ancient model that predates the law. It has a pile of old, light-bleached, colored poster board on top, bought to make scientific posters, some of the boards still in loose brown paper bags, and perched on top of that stack, the lab's Rock'em Sock'em Robot set. The little plastic boxing arena for the robots is roped in with yellow yarn that looks like a home fix and not the original accouterment. At one point, bizarrely, somebody attaches a large purple-and-red clay penis to one of the robots. Occasionally, visitors to the lab glance up at it and say nothing, carefully scrubbing all expression from their faces.

To the other side as the refrigerator, directly to the left as you look in the door, you'll see a chalkboard filling up much of the wall. I don't remember anyone ever using that chalkboard, except once when Tirin and Charlotte wrote down a bet about how, in Tirin's prediction, Charlotte would eventually leave the US for England. Tirin won the bet.

The garbage cans are lined up under the chalkboard, three in a row against the cinderblock wall. They're small, rectangular metal cans with rounded corners, painted a solid blue, rusty at the bottom, possibly corroded by lunch liquids. As strange as it is to be fond of garbage cans, I like them, because they epitomize the weird and shabby, 1960s personality of the lab. Like some kind of unintentional art deco.

Once, Hillary spends a week making a scientific poster to her exacting aesthetic standards for an upcoming meeting of the Society for Neuroscience. Like most good scientists, she is neurotic about the quality of her work. When it is done, she lays out the panels on the lunch table for the glue to dry overnight. Early the next morning, when the janitor comes through to wax the floor, he puts the garbage cans on the table, on top of the poster, leaving an imprint of rust and leaked Chinese sauces. Hillary is devastated and has to remake the poster. Just one of the challenges of science that you don't learn about in a textbook.

Charlie says that every lab needs a lunchroom. When he was designing the lab in 1969, he forgot the lunchroom, and at the last moment, the architect convinced him that he needed a space for people to gather and bond over food. The room was originally a single, cavernous area for experiments. But on the architect's advice, it was subdivided by a plasterboard wall, creating a small experiment room (eventually called the awake room) and a separate lunchroom. It's a strange and lovely arrangement, profoundly chaotic, because to get to the awake room, you must wheel your equipment and your supplies and your monkeys and all the accompanying filth *through the lunchroom*, often right past people eating lunch. Take that, health and safety. When I first join the lab, we live in an era of regulatory innocence.

You might reasonably wonder if a monkey will throw poo at the lunch table, as he is being wheeled past. The answer is, no, monkeys don't throw. It's a common misconception. Chimpanzees may be able to throw, and capuchin monkeys might learn it when trained by people, but our little gray fascicularis monkeys? Never. They can catch beautifully. If you toss them a treat, they can snatch it out of the air with precision. Maybe they are built to catch juicy insects. But the concept of a ranged weapon, of aimed throwing, is beyond their limited intelligence. In the course of studying how the brain orchestrates hand-eye coordination, we once trained a monkey to play a version of table hockey, but we could never get him to pick up and throw anything. Mr. Garrison does tend to distribute his poo, which excited us initially, but on closer study turned out to be an accident rather than an act of monkey genius. He gets the poo on his hands, dislikes the feel, and then flicks his fingers to get it off. It splatters like crazy, but he doesn't do it on purpose. We wisely never bring Mr. Garrison through the lunchroom.

Set against that plasterboard south wall of the lunchroom, to the right of the awake room door, stands a pastel, puke-green, metal, floor-to-ceiling bookcase. A crucial brain atlas lives on that bookcase—a set of photocopied pages in a black three-ring binder, a visual guide through every millimeter of the *Macaca fascicularis* brain. I know it well. For a while it's my bible. I study it, learning my way around the brain, and I'll forever remember the curls and patterns of its pictures like a child remembers a favorite Dr. Seuss book. Let's study the brain! Let's study on a train! Let's study on a plane! Let's study with champagne! I now know the monkey brain far better than I'll ever know the human brain. I can close my eyes and see every part of it in my head. If a pin enters the brain at the frontal pole and exits through the cerebellar vermis, name twenty major structures it passes through, in order. I can do that—I will always be able to do that—but only for the brain of a fascicularis monkey.

Along with the monkey brain bible, the bookshelf also contains a big, square, green, cloth-bound atlas of the cat brain, and next to it, an even bigger, gray, cloth-bound atlas of the rat brain. More is known about the rat brain, micron by micron, than the brain of any other mammal, and therefore it makes sense that the rat has the biggest atlas. Someone has left a steel, stereotaxic device for rat surgery sitting on the shelf next to the atlases. It might have come from Bart's lab—we don't do rat surgery in our lab. It looks like something for measuring shoe sizes, or like a modernist bookend. Next to it we have a model of the brain stem, made of a white, rubbery plastic that has become gray with dirt—a result of too many grubby-fingered people handling it. Someone has used red clay to fashion blood vessels on the base of the model, recreating the Circle of Willis. Other than these few items arranged in a line on one shelf, like a museum display, the entire metal bookcase is empty.

The lunchroom is my first office and it makes me feel like a grownup. I'm just a kid—I'm nineteen—when Charlie generously sweeps his hand toward a desk in the southwest corner of the room, tucked partly under some looming blue-green wall cabinets, squeezed beside the refrigerator, and proclaims that it's mine. I eagerly move in, filling the metal drawers and laminated desktop with photocopied neuroscience papers and books. At the back of the desk, pushed against the wall, I've arranged a sideways cardboard box filled with green terrycloth towels, a space for the baby monkeys to play and sleep. I don't think I'm supposed to bring the babies out of their nursery room, but I don't care. I like to give them exciting adventures, and Barney spends a lot of his time on my desk exploring or sleeping while I'm studying. I spend my time reading about the brain and, when nobody's looking, writing fiction. The noisy refrigerator motor clatters in my ear, and every day at noon I have to put down my work as the entire lab crowds in for lunch.

The lunch scrimmage takes place around a pale, Formica-covered table with silvery, tarnish-spotted legs, in the center of the room. It's really two tables pushed together, to fit the whole mob of us as we talk and argue and politick, sitting in mismatched chairs stolen from around the department. Earl and Seamus find some juicy chairs sitting unused in a corridor, somewhere in the public part of the building, and smuggle them back to the lab. The chairs are elegant, modern, beautiful, probably expensive. Each one is made of a single, cleverly curved, shining chrome pipe that doubles back on itself to form the frame of the chair. A wide, padded seat and back are bolted to the chrome frame. The fabric is wool-white, but after a week parked around our lunch table, it becomes rather badly stained. General Cho's red magic sauce, yogurt, Hoagie Haven catsup, hot sauce from Chuck's chicken wings, Coke, tea, coffee. The indentations where the buttons are affixed collect crumbles of food.

Bernie, the building manager, rampages into the lab during lunch and starts to shout. "Where did those chairs come from? Who stole them? They were bought for someone else! They're not for Charlie's lab! Get your feet off and get out of them! You carry them right back up to . . . Oh my God! Look at them! They're ruined! We CAN'T give them back! Shit! What's wrong with you people?" She storms out. We sit in shock, our sandwiches still partway to our mouths. It's funny in retrospect, but at the time, we grimace at each other guiltily. I don't know why I feel guilty—I didn't steal the things. We never do give them back.

Charlie almost always takes a big plastic vat of yogurt out of the fridge, that he eats with his particular large metal spoon, the yogurt getting in his beard. Once, in an attempt at imitation, the new Chinese student, Albert, brings in a plastic vat of sour cream and spoons it into his mouth, probably wondering how Americans can eat such crap. Sometimes we buy gigantic long subs from Hoagie Haven. (We have a monkey named Hoagie Haven.) When I take the 18-inch hoagie out of the white paper sleeve, I rip open the paper end-to-end and flatten it on the table as a kind of plate, to contain the mess of shredded lettuce and catsup. Sometimes we buy a lab pizza in a large white cardboard box, from Pizza Escort. (We have a monkey named Pizza Escort.) Seamus likes mushrooms. I like anchovies. Davidson's, the supermarket, is just down the street, and you can always buy your own sandwich material and a two-liter bottle of Coke. Sometimes we get buffalo wings and greasy potato salad from Chucks Café. (We have a monkey named Chucks.) We talk about food and politics and data. Earl and Linda have an argument about how large a typical horse penis is.

On Fridays, Hunan Take-Out has a lunch special. (We have a monkey named Hunan.) Earl often takes our orders and walks the five blocks to pick them up from Elsie, the friendly and maternalistic woman who runs the restaurant. She knows him and greets him by name. We each get an aluminum, compartmented plate with fried rice, General Cho's Chicken, and sautéed broccoli. The aluminum is almost too hot to handle as we pry the cardboard off the top. Scented steam billows up. Seamus loves the broccoli, especially when it's covered in General Cho's sauce. (Earl has a cat named General Cho.) All of us look forward to the Friday Chinese lunch except Charlie, who cheerfully derides the food in a booming voice. As an epicure and Sinophile, he is snooty about Chinese cuisine and condemns our food as garbage. But he's also perfectly happy to sample large amounts of it off our plates, while condemning it.

When we sit around the table we look like hippies displaced in time. All the men have long scraggly hair and beards. We have loose T-shirts and jeans, sneakers and sandals, loud voices and political opinions.

Charlie likes to tell us about his adventures in China, especially about real Chinese food and real Chinese restaurants, not the fake ones for tourists. You bring your own chopsticks in your pocket, or you'll have to use the communal ones stuck in a metal container of dirty water at the center of the table.

You reach across the table instead of passing dishes, and you spit the bones on the floor. You never eat all the rice, which is considered a sign that the hosts didn't put out enough food. I wonder how much of that narrative is true, how much is an idiosyncratic experience he had on one of his travels, or just his own exaggeration.

One day during lunch, I plop Barney the monkey on the table and let him go wild. Everyone is laughing. He's only about six months old, a little guy about the size of a regular brown and gray tree squirrel, squealing in excitement and leaping around as if his thin legs and arms were made of springs. He grabs at someone's banana. He thrusts his hand into a cup of apple juice and scoops up handfuls into his mouth in a sloppy splash. Everyone loves it. He's the life of the party until the government inspectors from the USDA walk in. They enter the front door of the lab and walk right past the wide-open door of the lunchroom without glancing in. When they disappear deeper into the lab, Seamus comes running back and hisses at me, "Get that monkey out of here!" Hillary runs in bearing a lab coat, gloves, and face mask, so I can look like I'm doing something official to the monkey. And so we escape a debacle. The lab could have been shut down forever had the inspectors seen a monkey on the lunch table. Is that not a sad truth?

When Tirin joins the lab, he and I make a bet. I'm applying to NASA for a fellowship. I'm hoping that, since I work on how the brain processes space (the space around the body within reaching distance), the NASA people might get confused and think I'm referring to the space up there with the planets. Or maybe they'll think my work relates to the interior design of a spaceship. Anyway, I apply, and I'm pretty sure I won't get that money. Tirin is sure I will. The prize: fifty chicken wings from Chuck's Café. Happily, Tirin wins. I earn the fellowship. Now here he is, sitting alone at the lunch table, pigging out on his fifty wings, hunched over an enormous silvery takeout tin, red grease and satisfaction on his face. He's outraged when I ask if I can have some. They're *his* wings. He's the one who fricken won the bet. I don't get a single one of them.

Once, Shalani's whole extended family—parents, siblings, smiling grandmother and frowning grandmother—are in the lunchroom, visiting, when I wheel Nirvana through, *en route* to his daily experiment. Normally, we don't like outsiders to see the monkeys because both sides can freak, but everyone here is cool. Her dad insists that Nirvana smiles at him, which is probably true—a monkey version of a smile is a shy, submissive grin, a flash of teeth.

Nothing stays the same. Later, in the final years of the lab, the lunchroom is cut by a cubicle-style partition running right through the space where my first office used to be, ruining it. You can see it in Figure 2. It violates my mental model of the lab and I never quite accept the modification. The new graduate students requested it. It's a four-inch thick, white, plastered slab, about head height, put in to make a semi-private stall for Charlotte and Maz, who set up an office behind the partition. You can get around the partition through a gap at its left end. Several desks are slid into the narrow space and parked underneath the overhanging green-blue cabinets. The cubicle wall itself collects stacks of books and papers piled on its flat plastered top, flopping over the sides.

I think Charlie, like me, has trouble accepting the violation of the old lab order. The lab is his house, after all, and has been so for thirty years. The lunchroom used to be the heart of the lab and mutilating it to accommodate the new graduate students must rankle in his soul. We buy a new color printer for the lab but don't unpack it immediately. It sits in its box on the lunch table for a few days until Charlotte and Maz unpack it, move it behind their wall, and set it up for themselves. When Charlie finds out that the new printer has been squirreled behind the wall, he blows up. When he loses his temper, he's so visibly invested in the emotion and shouts so forcefully— not loudly, but with emotional intensity—that it looks like his teeth are about to fly out of his mouth. I can't believe he's really angry about the printer. He could have just told them to move it to a more convenient location and share it with the rest of the lab. No, I'm pretty sure he's had a rising temperature, a pain and resentment around his heart, watching the new students commandeer his lunchroom and mutilate it with their crazy wall, taking away the social center of his lab, and the resentment has finally burst out of him. Sure, we can still eat in the lunchroom, in the little bit of it left to us, but it isn't the same. It's cramped, uncomfortable, and you never know who's lurking behind the wall, listening to your conversation. I understand Charlie's perspective perfectly.

7

THE AWAKE ROOM

Everyone calls it the awake room, which sounds like a comment on the alertness of the experimenters. In the old days, the lab studied the brain activity of anesthetized monkeys. It may seem odd to study a pickled brain, but it was the paradigm of the day. Anesthetizing a brain seemed to simplify it, make experiments easier, remove the complicating factors, or at least so people thought. Labs around the world relied on it. Then, in the 1980s, just before my time, Charlie's lab dipped its toes into the awake-monkey business. Among neuroscientists, the procedure came to be called the "behaving monkey paradigm," because the monkeys were trained to perform behaviors that could be quantified, like pressing buttons. But truthfully, the monkeys were not often well behaved, so we sometimes called it the misbehaving paradigm, and for a while the room was known as the misbehaving room. Which could have also referred to the humans, who were known to get amorous on occasion in the secret back rooms of the lab.

I could call it the Colombo room, because Colombo did experiments here for a while. Or the Cortical Stimulation room, because, years later, those were the last great experiments to come out of that perfect little space. It's probably most accurately called the Michael room, because I used it more than anyone else in its thirty-two-year span. It became my special scientific hermit cave.

Charlie says I'm a luddite. I never heard the word before he mentioned it to me, but I looked it up, and it means that I don't like new technology. Charlie always does have an uncanny intuition. He casually mentions something, and suddenly you realize just how far into you he's seen. It can be spooky. Am I really a luddite? I grew up on a farm in upstate New York, running around the fields and scrub and woods. I used to pretend I was a Robinson Crusoe castaway with a hatchet and a knife, and I'd make crude wooden shelters. My sister Lisa and I would go primitive and carve tools for ourselves. We even knapped stone tools like *Homo habilis*. We grew up with a wild animal's suspicion of towns, cities, crowds, cars, television, whatever it was that other people did. During summer vacation, for three months away from school, I never saw a TV or the inside of a car.

So for me to come out of the pure bright sunshine of the open wilderness into a cramped cinderblock bunker without natural light, surrounded by computers, may seem unlikely, or even torturous. But it isn't. It makes sense. Either I find myself a hidden den, or I connect to the public world—the crowds and parties and busy streets—and I'm not going to do that second one.

It does mean that I'm not a natural at technology. I'd rather walk than take a car. I'd rather read a book than use a computer. I'd rather solve a problem with duct tape and a wooden tongue depressor than with electronics and a software patch. For me to handle technology is like those awkward circus bears that learn to ride a bicycle. Well, circus bear it is. The life of a scientist requires learning your way around the technology, and, in the safety of the lab, I manage. All our equipment is homemade, so I had better know how to bolt, duct-tape, wire up, and program every bit of it.

Unlike every other door in the lab, the door to the awake room is cheap crap. It's made of flimsy, light, fake wood-stuff, grained and varnished. I believe one calls it a "hollow core" door. It has a cheap round doorknob, hollow brass, dented and knocked slightly crooked probably from someone trying to wheel equipment past it. The doorframe around it is also varnished wood, clumsily nailed into the wall with visible finishing nails.

When you walk in the door, the first thing you see, looming up on the left against the wall, is a tall equipment rack dripping with wires. An equipment rack is the centerpiece of any experiment, and in some ways becomes a matter of personal expression. Mine stands taller than my head. It has two vertical rails, made of gray galvanized steel, and attached to the rails, screwed in between them like rungs on a ladder, are various colorful pieces of equipment. The top two rungs are powder-blue panels that control the eye-coil machine. The next rung down is a silver controller for a juice valve that gives the monkey something sweet when he needs it. Next comes a black and red sound amplifier from Radio Shack that allows you to hear the sounds of the brain. Under the sound amplifier is a homemade electrophysiology amplifier, with its hand-lettered dials and switches and glowing red eye, a specialty device that can take the whisper-thin electrical signals from the brain and enhance them, pulling out the crucial frequencies. Lower yet, at a comfortable height such that I can use it when I'm sitting, I've rigged a small plywood surface, a tabletop, and I've placed my cathode ray oscilloscope on it. No, the oscilloscope is gone now. I had a beautiful, glowing-green cathode ray scope, an antique, a massive beast that weighed thirty pounds. Then it broke. It's been replaced by a cheap modern digital version, made of plastic, with a display that's jittery and hard on the eyes. Below the plywood surface I've placed the Schmidt trigger, a device that can take the jumbled electrical noise coming from the brain and isolate the one signal of an individual neuron. On the floor, at the base of the equipment rack, a loudspeaker sits in shadow in the corner. It's from a 1960s stereo set, I'm pretty sure. It's about a foot tall, wooden, painted blue with a brown coarse fabric over the front, and plays the sound of the brain picked up by the electrode.

The sound of the brain is hypnotic. It's structured static. Layers of hissing and rumbling, occasional popping as individual neurons leap up above the surface. Your ear gradually tunes into the nuance and it seduces you. I'm sure it sounds meaningless to a newcomer, but in time you become an old salt and can tell the weather from the sound of the waves.

In the middle of the room stands the functional heart, the island of the monkey—the rig itself. At the center of the rig is a simple wooden box, about two feet tall, painted white and turning gray from age and use. I think it was an equipment crate, or maybe a produce crate, that was repurposed as a monkey stool and set upside down in the middle of the room. It's securely fastened to the floor in grime and floor wax. Surrounding that box is a white plastic frame. The frame contains an induction coil that produces a weak magnetic field. We can use that field to measure the monkey's eye and head position. Around the plastic frame hangs a black felt drape that we close to give the monkey privacy, if he has trouble concentrating. Around the drape stands a scaffold of aluminum struts draped with wires, amplifiers, copper mesh—controlled chaos—reaching from floor to ceiling. That is what a 1990s monkey physiology rig looks like. Homemade. Crazed. Quirky. Lovely. If a monkey escapes in that room, which has been known to happen, he'll treat it like a jungle gym and go nuts tearing out wires, causing so much damage that it can take three days to fix it.

The room is like a sailing ship. It has no wasted space. You can barely move from one part to another, turning sideways and slithering past equipment, wires, shelves, computers, cluttered counter and sink and cabinets. Where an open space has been left, it always serves a specific functional purpose. I live in this room, navigating the brain, collecting data, analyzing data, programming equipment, embarking on one experimental voyage after the next, sometimes solo, sometimes with collaborators. I love the feel, the ship-shape feel, the sense of ownership, self-determination and exploration. One hand on the tiller and one on the sheet, an ear to the wind and an eye to the water—that is, one hand adjusting the microdrive by the subtlest of increments to move the electrode, one hand manipulating the knobs on the equipment to isolate the electrical signals of neurons, an ear to the crackling, hissing hash of electrical brain sounds, and both eyes consumed by the chop and ripple of green lines glowing across the oscilloscope screen. One or two larger signals pop up and my job is to coax them, nurture them, until they jump up through my two trigger dots, like getting a fish to jump into a net. In the dim room, the green lines are so bright and all-consuming that they take over my brain. They are a visual type of meditation mantra. I can sit for hours focused on the task. Sometimes, when science is frustrating and I can't seem to make headway, publications are thin and collaborators are difficult, I clear my mind of all the details, the future, the data and the people, and tell myself that the single most important event in the fourteen-billion-year history of the universe has finally come, and it is me, isolating one neuron, right now, right here. Nothing else matters. Catch the fish.

At night, when I close my eyes to go to sleep, I see green glowing oscilloscope lines twitching and vibrating. My brain has been reconfigured.

The awake room doesn't need any artistic decoration. The crazy wires and equipment filling every inch of space make their own aesthetic, like a Jackson Pollock painting. Nonetheless, on the inside of the brown wooden door, somebody, maybe Earl, maybe Seamus, has thumbtacked a poster of an orangutan baby. It's holding up both hands in excitement, smiling toothily, and sports a conical birthday hat strapped, slightly crooked, to its fuzzy head. The caption says, "Party Time!" Our monkeys, of course, are not orangutans. They're also not chimps—the ones that learn sign language. They're only little simians, and have a limited comprehension of the world around them. Tirin once described them dryly as "idiot savants, but without the savant part." They're fascicularis, sometimes called crab-eating macaques, or long-tailed macaques, although they don't grab anything with their tails, which are stiff and strictly for maintaining balance. They're about the size of a small dog, and in color and shape look like a tiny German Shepard with long legs, or a miniature baboon.

I'll risk explaining how we test the monkeys. Or at least, how we did it in the 1990s. I think the methods have moved on since I left animal research. Many people in the lab are wary of explaining our procedures to outsiders, because the pushback can be extreme. If you don't like the idea of animal experimentation, then you won't like my story, and I respect that. But I don't want to hide it. I think the hiding is a mistake and, itself, unethical. I urge you to think and feel your way carefully. If you have ever suffered from a disease, if you have a loved one who had cancer and needed the best available treatment, if you have ever urged for better health care for the country or thought that health care was a right—if you care about these things—then please remember that the entire medical universe rests on basic research, or research broadly into the body and brain. Not just targeted research meant to cure a specific disease, but the most fundamental research that asks: how does the biological machine work? That is the bedrock of all medical knowledge. And that's what we're doing here in the monkey lab. We're learning, one rare increment of insight at a time, about the basics of the brain and how it interacts with the body. If what I am about to tell you has some ick factor, please keep that larger goal in mind. I have no way to explain the lab, the essence of what we do, without explaining some of the procedures.

In an initial surgery, under anesthesia, the monkey has a cap attached to the top of his head. The surgery is an adaptation of a procedure often done on human epileptic patients to monitor their brain states. In the case of our monkeys, the cap is made of light but strong dental acrylic, which looks pink and lumpy like human gums. It looks like the monkey is wearing a hat made of carefully molded bubble gum, rising up out of the fur on his head. The cap contains two crucial components sticking out of the hardened bubble gum. First, it has a steel bolt by which we can keep his head still during the experiment, clamping it to a stabilization device. You cannot measure the activity of a single, microscopic neuron unless the head and the brain are nearly perfectly still. Second, the acrylic cap contains a small jar top made of stainless steel. The jar top is normally closed, but when we need to study the monkey's brain we can unscrew the flat metal disk, which is about an inch in diameter. Under it is skull with a small burr hole through which we can gain easy access to the cerebral cortex. After the head cap is attached, the monkey wakes up from surgery and recovers for a few weeks. We want him comfortable. We want him healthy.

Then the experiment itself begins. It's a daily task that can unfold over years. At the start of each day, you go to the colony room, coax the monkey into his Lexan chair, and wheel him on a cart down the corridors (and through the lunchroom) to the awake room. Along the way, his long stiff tail sticks out behind, slightly upcurved, and whacks your legs, which can be especially uncomfortable if the tail slips up beneath the hem of the lab coat and the loose open leg of your shorts, poking you in the private parts.

Once the monkey is in the awake room, we stabilize his head, open his jar top, and flush the inside with sterile saline. The procedure benefits from a bright surgical lamp shining down on the head. That's why the awake room contains a portable surgical lamp, like a brown metal giraffe with wheels on the bottom and an adjustable neck on top. When not used, it lurks in the corner, part of the immense but necessary clutter in the room.

Then—with a grunt of effort—you heave the monkey and his chair off the cart and onto the wooden box where he sits throughout the experiment. Heaving the monkey from the cart to the equipment rig is such a physical effort that it has become a moment of personal struggle for me. A daily moment of self doubt. I find myself pausing, taking a deep breath, wondering if I have the energy to lift the monkey, to do the experiment, to get through the day, to live, as if a grave-breath of philosophical horror has passed over me. Then I exert some muscle and hoist the monkey into position. Once I get over that hurdle, I feel better. I feel I can take on the rest of the day. It's a small moment that stands for the entire human endeavor, somehow. I give the monkey a treat, a bit of banana or a slice of apple, pet him on the back, talk to him, and he grunts understandingly. I have a rapport with him.

I know, I'm always talking about "he" and "him." Barney and The Mole and Mr. Garrison—they're all male. We do have females, but mostly they stay in the colony and liven up the monkey society. For the basics of sensory processing and movement control, it probably doesn't make a lot of difference if we study males or females. But their temperaments are different. Our species of monkey, the crab-eating macaque, has a strict male hierarchy. The big, chunky males with saber-like teeth are positioned at the top, and the young skinny males are at the bottom. You might think that a strong male with huge teeth is more dangerous, but they have a sense of hierarchy built so deep in their psychology that they intuitively respect and obey their human experimenters, who are, after all, five times their size. You can be as gentle as you like—the gentler the better—as long as you're calm and project confidence, and you'll soon develop your own rapport with the monkey, who will gladly do what he thinks you want. If you want him to press buttons, he'll press buttons. If you want him to reach here and there as you measure his arm movements, that's what he'll do. You teach him by giving him little rewards, raisins perhaps, or a squirt of apple juice when he does the right thing, and he soon gets the point. But reward only, never any negativity or you'll ruin your relationship with him.

The male monkeys also intuitively understand the hierarchy among us humans. They sense it like magic. If Charlie walks into the room to watch an experiment, the monkey, the disloyal little jerk, immediately transfers his allegiance from me to Charlie, smacking his lips in earnest submission, directing all his limited mental resources away from his task and toward the loud hairy alpha ape who is somehow obviously my boss. The experiment falls apart until Charlie looks up at the wall clock and says, sometimes around the dust of a cracker he's been eating, "Well, very good, Graziano, very good, carry on," and then cheerfully stumps out of the room.

The females, they have no sense of hierarchy. That's not how they evolved. They never accept you or anyone as boss, no matter how much bigger you are, no matter how confident you are, no matter what your status, and at least twice a week they'll have a go at ripping your face off. I know—I've tried to work with them, and they're just too independent-minded. I wouldn't call it rugged individualism. More like toothy psychopathy. It's in their nature. I'm not trying to say anything clever about human women. Humans are much less different between the sexes. This is just how *Macaca fascicularis* women are.

One of my favorite monkeys is Sequoia. He's calm and dignified, and his head is so large and strange-looking that Tirin says he looks like an Easter Island statue. His fur is yellow from the dusting of Nitrofurazone powder that we use to keep his jar top clean. He helps me discover a network of cells in the brain that keeps track of personal space. Every day he dances with the personal space machine. When he sits in the equipment, he faces west, toward the back wall. In front of him stands a massive steel table, an expensive piece of furniture with an adjustable top that you can raise or lower by cranking an iron handle. The table is painted flat black on its surface, gray on its undercarriage, and is heavy and sturdy, with wheels that can be locked in place. On it, I've set an industrial-grade robot that maneuvers an aluminum stick around the monkey. On the end of the stick is a ping pong ball wrapped up in orange tape, and the experiment requires the ball to move along specific, programmed trajectories through the monkey's personal space. Charlie and I name the robot René Descartes, because it's a cartesian format robot—you program it to move the ping pong ball in X, Y, and Z coordinates.

Nirvana the monkey is a nervous, wiry little guy who constantly drums his skinny hands on the plastic chair and loves his treats.

Nirvana is a juvenile monkey,
Who likes to drum out rhythms that are funky.
A bath he never took;
Instead he dribbles gook;
In consequence, he smells distinctly skunky.

I wrote that high-quality poem to amuse Lina, my lovely, funny, undergraduate assistant.

Nirvana helps us discover neurons in the cortex that keep track of nearby sounds, like when a mosquito suddenly zings past your ear and you want to flap it away. For that experiment, we use an enormous aluminum ring, about ten feet in diameter, suspended horizontally around the monkey. Speakers are mounted on aluminum poles at adjustable intervals around the ring, allowing us to test the auditory responses of neurons at precise angles. Jim Watson, our friend, the mechanical genius and shop guy, made that giant ring and the speaker holders. He loves it when I make drawings of the parts I need because he can gleefully ridicule my wobbly and smudgy draftsmanship. He begs me not to saw or drill any parts myself, and groans whenever he sees my handiwork. He says it looks like I carved it with my teeth. It's okay. I don't mind the ribbing, and I can kid back. Once, I dropped by his machine shop in the basement and stealthily left our rubber hand on his band saw table. I imagine it gave him a fright when he first saw it, but he never said anything. The hand just reappeared in the lab a few days later.

Terrance the monkey is the star of the awake room. He joins the team and shows us a crazy map of complex, useful movements in his motor cortex. The map was almost discovered 130 years ago—the first hints of it were described in passing— but then science took a detour and the truth was hidden until our own accidental discovery. Chance favors the prepared mind, they say. That's true. But far more important, in my experience: chance favors the mind that's not always friggin petrified of doing the wrong thing. You can't be afraid of the disapprobation of your peers.

We clear out the space in front of the monkey and arrange some chairs, including my favorite, wheeling, blue lab stool. The three of us—me, Charlotte, and Tirin—sit like a panel of judges, watching as we tickle parts of the monkey's motor cortex with microscopic amounts of electrical current. We have a big, bulky, ancient VHS video recorder, black, with a viewport that you have to put to your eye, and we use it to record the monkey's stimulation-evoked movements. One of us holds out a treat to entice the monkey's arm here and there, one of us holds the stimulation button—a red button on a rectangular piece of Plexiglas, connected to the equipment by a long black wire—and the third one holds the video recorder. Sometimes we perch the recorder in a stable location, such as on that black iron table. Usually I'm the scribe. I'm sitting with a black-bound notebook in my lap, scribbling in pen, describing and drawing quick sketches, getting ink stains on my fingers. Sometimes the monkey masturbates and grosses us out. Usually he's happy to get his raisins and apple pieces, enthusiastically interacting with us.

The experiment begins in 2001. I've been promoted to the faculty. I still feel like a newbie, a wide-eyed youth filled with endless enthusiasm for neuroscience. Every morning at seven, *every* morning, weekdays and weekends, holidays or not, Charlotte and I arrive. I prepare the equipment in the experiment room while Charlotte fetches Terrance from the colony. The two of us put monkey and equipment together and lower the electrode. When we hit first neurons, we let the brain rest for half an hour. By then, Tirin arrives, and the three of us study the brain.

You must understand the strangeness of what we're doing. Nobody imagined such a thing was possible. We dial in a site in the cortex and pipe in a whisper of current through the electrode for half a second at a time. Each time, like clockwork, the monkey closes his hand as if gripping something, raises his hand to his mouth, and opens his mouth as if receiving whatever he's gripping. He can't help it. He does it even though he has nothing in his hand. We've triggered a motor program.

Or, on another day, we dial in another site in the cortex and evoke a different, equally complex movement. A defensive outward thrust of the hand. Or a reach. Or a grasp. Or a climbing-like combination of arms, legs, and tail. The monkey's normal everyday actions are mapped out systematically on his motor cortex. It's a privileged look into how the brain organizes behavior. We work until noon and then wheel the monkey back home, but we don't ever stop arguing about what it all means. The results are so revolutionary that we can't agree. The conversations have an emotional intensity and a verbal light-speed rapidity. The three of us eat lunch together and argue. We eat dinner together and argue. We eat a lot of dinners at Theresa's Italian restaurant, until every waiter there gets to know us.

To me, that lovely room dies emotionally on one particular September day. That morning, Charlotte spends an extra-long time getting the monkey from the colony. I'm sitting in the experiment room waiting, wondering if she needs help. Did the monkey escape? Is he running around the colony room? Did Charlotte slip on a wet floor and hurt herself? It turns out that she's distracted by the news. The monkeys are supposed to be entertained by a TV in the colony room, though it's not clear they ever actually watch it. I don't think they have the cognitive sophistication to watch TV. Maybe it gives them some stimulating background noise. The animal caretakers often turn the channel to CNN so they can watch the news while mopping the floor. Charlotte, it turns out, is standing in the colony dressed up in her stained lab coat, blue mask, and green goggles, transfixed by the TV, watching a surreal series of events unfold in New York City. When she finally brings the monkey to the experiment room, wheeling him in on the cart, and pulls off her goggles and mask, she relays a confused story about planes hitting the World Trade Center. I don't know what it means, but I'm pretty sure it's an accident, one of those crash tragedies that happens every so often.

Then Tirin fails to show up for the experiment. He's in his office watching the coverage. After a while, Charlotte and I give up trying to keep our minds on the experiment. We close up, put the monkey back home, and join Tirin in front of his TV, watching the fall of the towers and other events around the country. Hours later, we begin to smell a foul, acrid smoke wafting over the state line to New Jersey. It's literally the smell of death. That smog contains the remains of incinerated people.

Somehow, after that day, we lose enthusiasm for the routine of the experiment. It doesn't seem important anymore. The results are published in 2002 in a paper coauthored by the three of us, a publication that has a profound ripple effect on neuroscience. But I can never shake the horrible association in my mind between that specific paper and the smell of dead people.

8

THE QUARANTINE ROOM

When new monkeys arrive in the lab, we keep them in quarantine for a month. But new monkeys are rare. I can go for years at a time and never enter the room; consequently, I have trouble remembering what's in it. Some free-standing monkey cages wheeled up against the west wall. Silvery, made of welded stainless-steel bars. I'm always surprised by the thinness of the bars—an eighth of an inch. I can't even remember if there's a sink in the room. That's how poor my sense of the place is. There might be a stainless-steel sink, or there might not. I'll have to go look to refresh my memory. But not right now—I'm too comfortable in my sagging chair in the awake room, programming my equipment, bouncing my tennis ball against the cinderblock wall.

The quarantine room is weirdly long and narrow, with a tall ceiling. It's a slot, an architectural accident. Architecture really does have a direct line to human emotion. The shape of the room makes me feel subtly uncomfortable when I'm standing in it.

The room has an extra door at the back end. It's the same kind of aqua, solid wooden door that you see elsewhere in the lab. But this door, let's call it the postern, is a spatial anomaly. It's a wormhole, like in science fiction when you enter a black hole and come out somewhere else in the universe. If you were to leave by that postern, you'd encounter the massive pile of old equipment in the back hall. Presuming you could crawl over the pile, you'd be *outside the lab*. And right next to the bathroom at the back door. How weird is that? You'd be instantly transported from one part of the cognitive map to a different, distant part. If you look at Figure 1, you'll understand. To walk from the quarantine room to the back hall should entail passing up Corridor A, turning left, passing along most of Corridor B, turning left again, passing down to the back door, and leaving the lab. The route is the longest possible path through our world, and yet an anomaly directly connects these two most spatially distant points. It's a geometric paradox.

I've never once seen that door opened, and have never known or heard of anyone passing through it. I don't even think of it as a door.

9

THE PREP ROOM

Social neuroscience didn't exist until the 1970s, when it crawled out from the dark warm nursery of the Gross Lab prep room. Long before my time, this room was the scientific heart of the lab. The legendary experiments took place here, including Charlie's famous discovery of face cells and biological motion detectors—the primordial origins of an entire modern field of study.

In the old days, you prepared a monkey (hence "prep") by anesthetizing it on a table, and then you studied the neural signals that wandered sluggishly through its sleeping networks. Anesthesia does not turn the lights out in the brain—it's more like a dimmer knob that turns it down but always leaves a little bit of oomph. It allows you to study a simplified version of the brain reduced to its most basic information-processing framework. That's the theory, anyway. Only some areas of the brain, like sensory processing areas, can be usefully studied in that preparation. As for the rest of the brain—the thinking part, the deciding part, the feeling part—it goes dark when the monkey is asleep. Or, as Charlie puts it, the cerebral cortex is "soluble under anesthesia."

My account of the prep room comes from my earliest years in the lab. Anesthetized preps, still performed in the late 1980s, went extinct during the 1990s, and after that, the prep room became largely a ghost room full of obsolete, dusty equipment. Everything I describe here, therefore, must be understood through the lens of ancient history.

My earliest memories of the prep room are of a huge windowless cave smelling faintly of leaked anesthesia and more strongly of monkey, filled with mysterious equipment racks and wires and blue-green cabinets looming out of the shadows.

My first day in the lab, I'm allowed to watch an experiment. I've never encountered science like this before. I'm listening to the clicking, scratching sounds of neurons inside a brain in real time. It's astounding. It's world-altering. It's especially startling when the monkey's brain starts to swear and complain about the traffic—a consequence of the electrode picking up the CB radio transmissions from truckers on Route 1.

Soon I become a useful assistant, turning knobs, adjusting gas anesthesia as instructed, even writing in the fancy green-bound ledger that Charlie prefers to use as a data book. Charlie's handwriting is a dyspraxic scrawl, crooked but surprisingly readable when he makes the effort. Hillary's handwriting is a flowing, perfect cursive, like a foreign script, "linear H" I call it, difficult to decipher. My own block writing is like Charlie's, if a little less wiggly. When I write rapidly, and when Charlie writes carefully, the two samples become indistinguishable, a similarity that pleases me.

I beg Charlie to let me do my own experiments, even though I'm only an undergrad. He tells me that I need to think of something worthwhile, and I come back with the claustrum. It's a poorly understood part of the brain. I ask, "Can I please make tracks for the claustrum, study its neurons, and find out what kind of visual signals it processes? Can I? Can I?" We are, after all, a sensory lab equipped to study visual responses, and the claustrum is known to be connected to the visual system. Charlie gives the go-ahead, and Hillary, the brilliant, capable, and beautiful head post doc in the lab, coaches me. At the time, I don't fully appreciate the generosity. I accept it as though I'm entitled and plunge into the experiment. I definitely have more than a pinch of youthful arrogance.

Each anesthetized experiment starts in the morning, stretches into the evening, long past a normal bedtime, and ends only when the monkey recovers from the anesthesia by four or five AM. It's a grueling experience that I can manage only once or twice a week. But it's exciting. I've discovered the joy of pushing myself for a larger purpose. The harder the task, the more I want to prove myself against it. Sometimes I think of it like fire-walking. You have to show your nerve and walk across the glowing embers to get to the scientific truth on the other side. You have to be willing to sacrifice your own physical comfort.

I don't even know how much time I've clocked in the middle of the night, sitting in one of the lab's green chairs, the vinyl upholstery on the arm rests sticking to my elbows, as I wait for a monkey to recover from anesthesia. My mind is reeling. I've squeezed it intellectually for most of a day, the slow leak of nitrous oxide into the room air has also befuddled me, and now I can do nothing more than exist in the moment. My mind fuses with the room around me. The space is huge, empty of people, full of equipment. Every bit of it becomes an extension of me, and it's always from this trippy perspective that I experience the room. *Let us go then, you and I, when the evening is spread out against the sky, like a monkey etherized upon a table.* I can't help thinking of the poem by T.S. Eliot whenever I'm in that room, in that mentally impaired state.

A furry brown monkey—Admiral Poindexter is my first— lies still, peacefully breathing, propped up in a sphinx position, his hands hanging off the front edge of the table in the center of the room, his long stiff tail stretching out behind. His eyes are open, covered with contact lenses to keep them moist and focused on a projection screen. The screen hangs from the ceiling in an elaborate, black-painted, iron structure, homemade and sturdy and serviceable. Under the monkey and around him I've tucked layers of padding—blue pads we call them—absorbent diaper material. Monkeys have a distinctive species smell. They stink, the blue pads stink, the whole room stinks, but you get used to it because, pretty soon, you stink too.

The table underneath him, the central altar of the prep room, is a cheap wooden thing with a hard, white, Formica top. It's riddled with drill holes of various sizes in seemingly random locations, the particle-board material of the table visible inside the holes. Charlie tells me that in the old days, before my time, he and his students used to argue for hours over where to put each hole. They're for mounting specific pieces of equipment, but whatever that old equipment might have been, we evidently don't need it anymore. We don't use the holes except for one purpose that I'll explain later.

Under the table, an electric respiration pump hisses and thumps, inflating and deflating Poindexter's lungs through a pink rubber tracheal tube protruding from his mouth. Charlie scrounged that rusty old, grease-smelling pump for free from a vet clinic. In the middle of the night, its rhythmic, heart-like thumping numbs my senses.

Charlie also managed to scrounge a free anesthesia machine, an army surplus unit originally from the Korean War and built for battle conditions. It's indestructible. It stands next to the table, a gaunt gray skeleton of metal, about four feet high on wheels. Air regulators and valves and a copper halothane canister hang from it like big colorful poppies clustering on a stalk. Its job is to take anesthesia gases from the metal air tanks that are chained up against the far wall, mix them in precise ratios, and send the mixture to the monkey.

You must look into the monkey's eyes to check whether they are correctly focused on the projection screen. You hunch in a low chair, holding the delicate ophthalmoscope, looming so close that you can smell monkey funk and a whiff of anesthesia leaking from the homemade gas fittings—the distinctive, unpleasant, sweetish tint of halothane and nitrous oxide. I've seen Charlie get so far up into the monkey's face that he bumps the snout and drenches his hands in monkey drool. Then—this is true—Charlie stabilizes himself by bracing his hands on the edge of the table and hooking his upper teeth on his drool-slimed knuckles. You're not supposed to swap saliva with monkeys because they can carry horrific diseases. The common monkey version of herpes, it turns out, is almost always fatal to humans. It's hard to catch, maybe one in a million, but if you drink their saliva, you probably improve the odds. Charlie doesn't mind. Risks don't seem to enter into his head. He isn't macho; he's so focused on what interests him at the moment that everything else fades away from his attention.

I can imagine Charlie, younger, thinner, redder in hair, sitting around this same wooden monkey table with the mythical heroes of the past, like Dave Bender, Charlie Bruce, Eric Schwartz, Ricardo Gattass, Bob Desimone, Tom Albright, close to the beginning of time as far as I'm concerned, designing the equipment, drilling holes in the table, discussing what stimulus to try next. They would have sat in the same green and blue and tan lab chairs behind the rear-projection screen, in the dark, shining spots and slits of light with a hand-held projector for the benefit of a peacefully sleeping monkey. They would have used the same projector that I'm using, made by Dave Bender out of scrap metal, a few cheap lenses, a bulb, and a fan from a hair dryer, held together with duct tape. It gets so hot that I have to hold it wrapped in a surgical towel.

Here is a moment famous in science—one of Charlie's stories, not mine. He and his students were studying a particular neuron, listening to it click. They could not figure out what drove it. The clicking was random, a few times a second, and nothing they did seemed to affect it. They shined images on the screen, spots and colors, lines and circles, and the neuron refused to react. In a rage of determination, they studied the neuron for hours and could not make it respond. Finally, reluctantly, they gave up and said goodbye to the cell, waving at the monkey's face, and in that moment the cell fired off an enthusiastic burst like a batch of firecrackers. It turned out the neuron responded only to the sight of a hand. And that neuron was the beginning of a new field of neuroscience, the first glimmer of how the highest levels of perception operate and how vision makes contact with social intelligence.

You don't get moments of discovery like that very frequently. Once a lifetime, maybe. If you're Charlie, four or five times. Most of the time, you're collecting data that doesn't gel into any sort of sense. You're combing through past literature, reading photocopied papers until your fingers turn black with ink, trying to find out if anyone else encountered the same patterns and made sense of them. Or you're arguing with your colleagues with mounting frustration, each of you convinced that the others must be idiots for not seeing the point. Or you're writing, struggling to take something absurdly complicated that you only just understood yesterday and turn it into a simple, inevitable, linear account. Or you're struggling with broken equipment. A casual observer might look at our homemade rigs filled with tangled rat's nests of wires and wonder how the equipment ever works. But if you buy your equipment ready-made, factory produced, it'll look pretty, it'll break, and you won't be able to fix it because you won't know how it's put together. Always build your own.

Electrical noise is the bane of the neurophysiologist. Not just CB radios on Route 1, but the constant hum of the wall current gets into the equipment and swamps out the delicate signals from the brain. Every experiment requires hours of tweaking, running wires here and there to try to ground the devices, wrapping copper mesh around this or that amplifier: try it now, how about now, what about now? And the copper rail. I can't ignore such a peculiar aesthetic feature. It runs around the prep room at waist height (and the awake room and the lunchroom, for that matter). It looks like a flat lath, about an inch tall and a quarter inch thick, mounted about an inch in front of the wall, held in place by little metal posts and screws. It's a bit dingy, blackened in places, but if you scratch it with a paperclip, you'll uncover the bright color of real, pure copper. You'd be forgiven for assuming it's art deco, something the architect put in to give the room a dash of character against the dull, beige, painted concrete. But it's a grounding strip. You wire your equipment to it, to ground out unwanted electromagnetic fluctuations.

Fluorescent lights are the worst for noise, generating waves of invisible disruption that ripple through amplifiers and electrodes. They are banished from the prep room. The ceiling lights, glowing disks the size of car tires that hang from the ceiling, are filled inside with incandescent bulbs. Brian, a new member of the lab and an eager young undergraduate, is standing on a chair changing a bulb. Charlie and I are sitting nearby. A monkey is sleeping on the table. I don't know what unwholesome sense of humor stirs inside me, but I say, casually, as Brian's hand is groping in the light fixture, "Remember the guy who touched the wires on top of the train?" It's a famous Princeton tragedy. Charlie gives me a ferocious, quelling look, one of the few times I've ever seen him angry at me. It's a cutting moment for me, and also a lesson. Never disrespect the new students. The lab, science itself, is always about the new students.

Another time, I almost blow up the lab. I'm exhausted, alone with the anesthetized monkey in the early hours of the morning, nearly done with my work, waiting for the animal to wake up so I can make sure he's okay before putting him back in his home cage. I've turned on an electric heater to keep him warm in the meantime. The boxy brown heater sits on the floor near the monkey's table, on little metal feet, its coils glowing red inside. Without realizing it, I've stretched the green rubberized oxygen tube across the floor, from the gas tanks to the monkey, directly past the front of the heater. Suddenly a sparking, hissing, flaming sound erupts from that corner of the room. The heat has melted a tiny hole in the oxygen line, pure oxygen is gushing directly into the front grille of the heater onto the red-hot coils, and the room may be seconds from exploding for all I know. If flame travels up the inside of the tube to the big metal oxygen tank against the wall, the tank could blow up like a bomb. I have no idea if that's possible, but the scenario springs into my head and, from a comfortable drowsiness in the heated air, I've snapped instantly into jangling wakefulness. I leap out of my chair, run across the room, and twist close the valve on the oxygen tank. No problem. A good neurophysiologist can master a great range of skills, including how to avoid death by explosion. Fortunately, we have an extra oxygen hose coiled in a drawer, and in about a minute (while the monkey breathes room air) the equipment is working again.

When an experiment is done, the neurons tested, the data collected, and all that remains is to recover the monkey, I have no choice but to sit and wait alone, hour after hour, through the most surreal part of the night. What can I do to fill the time? I've tried writing fiction or music; but when I'm accidentally stoned on leaked halothane and nitrous oxide, complex creativity doesn't come out well. Instead, I invent brainless games to pass the time, and the best game my drugged brain has ever invented is the Q-tip Olympics.

We use surgical-grade, extra-long cotton swabs as part of our toolkit. Each swab has a thin, pine-wood handle, about six inches long, and a small, tightly wrapped ball of cotton attached to one end. I take an old, partly-used package, whose sterility has been compromised already, pull out a cotton swab, and insert the back end into one of the holes drilled into the wooden surface of the monkey's table. I told you these holes have a use. By trial and error, I've found exactly the right hole for the procedure. I insert the swab only a third of an inch, then gently bend it back toward me like a miniature catapult, generating tension. When the swab is curved back as far as I think it can go without breaking, I let go. It springs forward, flies out of the hole in the table, and arcs end-over-end across the room directly toward the sink, about fifteen feet away.

If I finesse the flick just right, I can get the cotton swab to land right in the sink. If I'm lucky, I might even get it to arc higher. One point for the sink, three for the metal shelf just above the sink, four for the next shelf up, and five points on that rare flick, one in a hundred, when the swab soars beautifully into the highest shelf, just beneath the ceiling. New swabs are too brittle and often break when I try to bend them. Swabs that have been put through the steam sterilizer too many times are soft—the wood has gone soggy. But swabs that have been sterilized once and have since dried out are perfect. I'm the world champion and sole participant in this particular sport, having expended at least a hundred hours of my life and thousands of cotton swabs in a daze of obsessive confusion.

I wake up suddenly to the voices of my mother, father, and grandmother, talking quietly among each other. They are not quite next to me, maybe through a door, maybe in the next room over. I open my eyes a crack, just enough to get a blurry sense of where I am. The light from the window tells me right away that I'm in my childhood bedroom in Buffalo, and I close my eyes again. But I can't remember how I got here. The last I remember, I was finishing an experiment in the prep room, but then the images grow hazy.

The voices are just outside the bedroom door, and I can hear them with great clarity. I'm wide awake now and listening intently. I gather that I've been in a coma for at least a year, possibly a decade—they don't come right out and say how long. The best I can figure, the anesthesia in the prep room must have finally gotten to me and overwhelmed my brain. Maybe I had a stroke. Somebody must have found me the next day, unresponsive on the floor, and eventually, after a hospital stay, I was transported to my parents' house where they've been caring for my comatose body ever since.

My grandmother must have a cane now, because I can hear it thumping as she walks closer, opens the door to the bedroom, and approaches the bed. Maybe every day they try gentle stimulation to rouse my brain. Whatever the reason, my grandmother continues to thump the floor with her cane, right beside the bed. Thump, thump, thump. I keep my eyes closed, afraid to open them and face whatever my medical reality may be. I'm terrified. My parents are now talking quietly about a nurse who, apparently, visits and cares for me three times a week. I can't help but notice that, for an old wobbly lady, my grandmother has an impressive sense of rhythm. Her cane thumping is machine perfect. Suddenly suspicious, I open my eyes a little more than a crack, just enough to see properly. I'm in the prep room, alone, lying on the cot; the monkey is anesthetized in front of me; the thumping is the respiration pump; and nobody is talking. The voices, which were perfectly clear in my ear, have instantly shut off. I realize, looking at the wall clock, that I dozed off less than ten minutes ago.

That's what the prep room can do to you in the middle of the night. It fucks with your brain, dude.

Anyway, I shouldn't be sleeping on that uncomfortable aluminum-frame cot. It has a dirty old mattress about an inch thick, wrapped up in someone's unwashed sweat-stained sheets. You need to drape the mattress with a lab coat before taking a nap on it, because the monkey shit on the lab coat is less of a disease vector. The official purpose of the cot is for resting during long experiments, but honestly, it's more often used for clandestine sex and eventually the pounding breaks the back legs of the thing.

The prep room is so large that it supports several different ecosystems: the sink ecosystem, the cabinet ecosystem, the monkey rig ecosystem, and the far-back-of-the-room ecosystem. A table is set near the back of the room against the south wall, the wall with pipes running along the bottom. An old boxy computer on the table is already scientifically obsolete, and has only one remaining use—it runs an ancient game with bad graphics called *Dangerous Dave and the Haunted Mansion.* The game is addictive and sweeps the lab for a while. I spend hours sitting at that table, working assiduously on killing zombies and knife-guys with my pump-action shotgun, feeling worse and worse, grimmer and darker, because, even though I'm only murdering pixelated monsters, the hamburger-meat carnage has a subtle, corrosive effect on my emotions. I cannot get farther from my old life, running barefoot through fields and scrub in the wilderness, than sitting in a windowless bunker playing a bad, but addictive, shooter video game in the dark, waiting for a monkey to recover from anesthesia.

It's 1990. I'm a graduate student at MIT, in Boston. I've left Princeton, for now. I've left Charlie's lab, sort of, but I'll never completely sever that bungee-cord connection. Every weekend I commute to Princeton by train to do experiments. I wake up at four in the morning on a Saturday, stumble outside, like as not in the snow, take the subway to the Amtrak station, catch a train, sleep a little if I can, and arrive at Princeton by lunch to start an all-night experiment. Now it's Saturday evening. Charlie and I are sitting in the prep room near the anesthetized monkey, Glenfiddich, who is stretched peacefully on the table. The whole lab is empty, quiet. An hour earlier, Charlie brought dinner from Chez Alice—savory dishes in plastic containers—and we've already eaten. Yes, we've eaten next to the anesthetized monkey. I don't mean we put our dinner on the same diaper pads as the monkey—we're not savages—I mean we stripped off our latex exam gloves and ate with plastic forks on the nearby countertop. The room still smells like French food, masking the monkey odor and the fainter whiff of anesthesia. When Charlie brings food, he goes gourmet. We're not going to end up with pizza or sandwiches.

Now Charlie has my data book on his knees and a stub of pencil in his hand. With Charlie, pencils break a lot because he tends to use too much pressure. We're studying a brain structure called the putamen, listening intently to the sound of a single, microscopic neuron over the loudspeaker. When the neuron generates a faint spark, its way of signaling to its neighbors, the electrode tip picks up that tiny release of energy, relays it to our amplifier and boxy brown stereo speaker, and we hear it as a loud click. Normally the neuron clicks now and then, once every few seconds. If we present a visual stimulus—I'm waving a ping pong ball on the end of a long rod, and Charlie is brandishing a bright green toilet brush from the stimulus drawer—the neuron responds. The clicking suddenly speeds up, like a machine gun, firing at perhaps fifty clicks per second, but only when the stimulus is thrust into the left side of the monkey's personal space. Somehow, one side of the visual world is wired up to this neuron and the other side is not.

We put a black felt blindfold on the monkey. With his eyes blocked, the visual response is gone, of course. But when we lean close and touch the monkey's left hand, the instant we bend even a single hair, the neuron fires up again like a machine gun. Stop touching, and the neuron drops back to its calm baseline. Touch anywhere else on the body than the left hand, and we get no reaction.

"It's amazing! It's sensational!" Charlie says, his hair and beard quivering from enthusiasm. His lips must be twitching. "Do it again! Try it again! Wait, I'll close my eyes and try to tell you what you're doing. You're touching him! Now! No. No. Now! That's not a touch! That's a visual response—it's not as strong. I can tell! You can't fool me!"

Charlie and the anesthesia in the room air are antipodal. With Charlie in the room, I can't help but feel entirely awake and jazzed up by his energy.

We have here a neuron that takes in two kinds of information: vision and touch. What's it doing? Why does it combine two seemingly unrelated information streams?

"Um, Charlie," I say, "What if we move the hand?"

He smiles. Charlie's smiles are always amplified by the movement of the bristles around his mouth. He sees immediately what I mean. The monkey's hands are limp, dripping off the edge of the table in front of him, his right hand about five inches to the right of his snout, his left hand five inches to the left. We prop his left hand in a new position, gently slanting it across his midline until it dangles on his right side. I wave the ping-pong-ball wand around the monkey's body again. Now, instead of responding to the sight of the ball on his left side, the neuron responds only to the sight of the ball on his right side. The visual response has moved, dragged along with the hand. The eyes haven't moved. The head hasn't moved. Only the arm has moved, and the visual response is glued to the hand.

We try another trick. We move the left arm again, this time tucking it back out of sight along the side of his body. Now, when we wave the magic ping pong ball on a stick, the visual response is gone. With the hand tucked away, out of sight, the neuron no longer responds to any visual input.

This neuron, it turns out, is like a radar telling the brain when something is either near or touching the left hand. It combines vision and touch, but it also incorporates information about the joint angles that define the position of the arm. It binds together a vast amount of information to arrive at a simple, important piece of news for the brain: something external is near or touching my left hand!

We don't realize that we've just shared a moment of profound discovery. Sure, it's a lovely observation, but we have no idea that it will ripple out and change the way neuroscientists think about the brain. You search and work and obsess, you spend years in the lab and hopefully enjoy yourself along the way eating French food and pizza, you publish journal filler hoping somebody will find it interesting or at least it will help your career, and then one day you find a tiny little crystalline piece of new truth, something that matters. That's how science works.

Later in the evening, Charlie goes home and I'm alone. I study a few more neurons, finish the experiment for the night, put away the equipment as the monkey sleeps peacefully on the table. When he can breathe on his own without the respiration pump, I carry him gently back to his home cage. When I'm finally done, the prep room cleaned, the counters wiped, the floor swept, the gas tanks turned off, it's four o'clock, Sunday morning. I have a long time to wait for my train to Boston. It's a good idea for me to get some rest because I have been known to stumble outside in a daze of exhaustion, get on the wrong train, and wake up unexpectedly in Washington DC, Union Station. I pull on my winter coat and walk for twenty minutes in the bitterly cold darkness, crunching through the snow, to Charlie's house on Woodside. He's left the front door unlocked for me. I creep in quietly, head to the guest room on the ground floor, and collapse on the bed to get a few hours of sleep.

10

THE COMPUTER ROOM

At the back of the prep room, you'll find a secret door, a folding door, an accordion-style, plastic, beige part of the wall that you barely notice in the shadows.

Usually the accordion door is not pulled fully closed. A dark gap remains. When I work in the prep room on experiments, I don't like that gap, and have a weird compulsion to close it. You need to put some muscle into it to stretch the accordion folds, until the metal latch reaches its counterpart on the wall, and you need to jiggle the old, failing mechanism to make the two pieces click together, the metal hook falling into place in the correct slot. When I start an experiment in the prep room, one of the first items on my checklist is to close and latch that back door. You don't know what bear or snake lives in the back crevasses of your home cave. I think it's a primordial fear, an instinct wired into me. Apparently, I'm the only one in the lab with that particular neurotic instinct.

Behind that folding door, in a small secret room, hidden like the Great and Powerful Wizard of Oz behind a curtain, lurks a massive computer. Originally, it was a PDP-12 computer, a refrigerator-sized processor, state-of-the-art, common among all high-end science labs. It was a 1960s machine with spinning reels of magnetic tape and blinking lights, running the complexities of experiments and storing data. I'm told that the old PDP-12 used to generate heat like a nuclear fire. On a cold winter day, if you felt chilled, you could sit in the computer room and warm right up. On a rainy day, you could dry off double quick. The heat was so overwhelming that a massive air conditioner was mounted on the ceiling. Two of them side by side, actually, some kind of special, industrial-strength model, cased in brown metal, hanging down about a foot from the ceiling, powerful enough to cool a cathedral.

Given the progress of technology, eventually the PDP-12 is replaced with a newer model. The company counts downward instead of upward—maybe a harbinger of its ultimate demise— and the next model is called the PDP-11. For a decade, the PDP-11 is the most elite laboratory machine available. The name trips off the tongue at conferences all over the world, as scientists compare notes. By the time I arrive in Charlie's lab in the late 1980s, however, the refrigerator-sized monstrosity of the PDP-11 is already obsolete. It's as quaint as a horse-drawn carriage and seems to be broken most of the time anyway, waiting for specialty parts that are no longer manufactured.

On the rare occasions when our PDP-11 becomes operational, it generates much less heat than its predecessor. We don't need the massive air conditioners anymore and usually keep them turned off, but now and then we take advantage of their enormous cooling power. When Charlie plans a pig roast in his backyard, we buy a whole gutted pig from a butcher shop, put it in a medical body bag, add a gallon of marinade, tie off the bag at the mouth with a cable tie, and store it in the computer room for a few days under refrigeration conditions, along with crates of cold drinks.

But you want to be careful where you put your food in that refrigerator. Always set it down on a clean chair, or on a garbage bag cut open to form a tarp. The computer closet is exceptionally dirty. When you step inside, you can feel and hear grit under your feet, probably because the janitor has never discovered that secret back room. It has not been swept or mopped since it was first built, decades ago. The corners have gone black from dust that has settled, turned into a paste, and petrified. A piece of white plastic strap is lying on the floor, cut from around a packing case of computer parts, and nobody ever bothers to pick it up and throw it out. It just stays there year after year like a weird piece of décor and crunches under your shoe if you step on it.

In the 1990s, the PDP 11 is carried out in state and tossed in a dumpster. The closet is refurbished and turned into an experiment room, and the accordion door is replaced with a solid wall. You can't reach the new space through the back of the prep room anymore, and must take another route. The computer room, with its industrial air conditioner and dirty floor and crunchy plastic strap, becomes the first part of the old lab to disappear from reality and slip into the world of memory.

11

THE DARKROOM

Hillary says, "I have a job for you."

I'm the new gofer, the paper towel guy, the undergraduate assistant. I say, "Okay, tell me."

She hands me a little white cardboard box. "In here," she says, in her whisper-quiet voice, "are 200 glass slides of a brain. Your job is to trace them onto paper. I'll show you how."

She leads me to the darkroom. Getting led into a dark closet by an attractive post doc inspires some interesting ideas, which I keep to myself for the time being, but this place is small, cramped, uncomfortable, unromantic, and I'm distracted by the weird equipment around me. The room has a red light on the wall so that you can see what you're doing without ruining your film. I've never been in a darkroom before, and I play with the light switch, turning it on and off, a goofy excess of enthusiasm that does not appear to amuse Hillary.

"Can we focus?" she says dryly.

Filling up most of the little room is a green plastic countertop with shallow basins. They're not sinks, of course, but baths for photographic plates. A blue lab stool fills up the tiny remaining floor space, and when I sit on the stool, there's not much room for my knees.

The plastic basins, not in recent use, are covered by a large sheet of plywood, giving an impression of archeological layers. I like the idea of working on a project while ancient, previous projects lurk in the alluvial layers beneath.

On top of the plywood, a strange, massive piece of equipment squats. It looks like a gigantic, medieval microscope that a monk built out of primitive materials. It fascinates me. Its base is a slab of varnished hardwood, maybe oak or maple, a hefty piece about three feet long, two wide, and a good inch thick. A metal tower rises up about three feet from the back part of the base. The tower has a bumpy, granular texture. It's probably iron and is painted flat black. Near the top of the tower, a lens points down at the slab of wood that forms the base. A few inches above the lens, metal rails hold a flat piece of glass about the size and shape of a standard sheet of paper. The glass is not fixed in; it can slide off its rails, and apparently has done so at least once because a crack runs diagonally through it. From above the glass platform, an exceptionally dim lightbulb housed in a collimator shines downward. The contraption is an enlarger. You put a specimen on the glass platform above, a sheet of white paper on the wooden platform below, and an image of your specimen, enlarged about ten times, appears on the paper, where you can trace it. But you need to put the machine in a dark place for that dim beam of light to reveal anything. Hence the darkroom.

I have my orders. I close myself into that tiny closet and start to trace brain sections. It's a good way to learn neuroanatomy. In the old days, apprentice composers learned their craft by copying music manuscripts. Just so, I'm learning the intricacies of the cortex. After five hours in the dark, I come stumbling out late in the afternoon, legs numb, eyes bleary, brain dazed, with a giant stack of paper in my arms, and hand it to Hillary.

She looks shocked, leafing through the pages to confirm that the drawings are detailed and meticulous. "Is *that* where you disappeared all day?" She shrugs, a faint trace of a smile flickering over her heavily lipsticked mouth. "I thought this project would last two months. Now I'll have to think of something else for you to do." I'm happy that she looks more impressed than annoyed.

The darkroom is eventually remodeled, turned into the control closet for the new experiment room. You can see it in Figure 2. When I stand in the corridor in front of the door, if it's closed, I have a weird, double perception—two realities flipping back and forth in my head. If I open the door and look in, will I find Hillary adjusting the ancient enlarger in the old dark room? Or will I find Tirin jumping around in enthusiasm in front of a stack of glowing monitors, watching the progress of his monkey? Like an experiment in quantum mechanics, both realities seem to exist at the same time until the door opens.

12

THE HISTOLOGY ROOM

Past the dark room you'll find the brightest room in the lab, the organizational nerve center, the door always open and the lights on. The lab technician—manager of all scheduling and ordering—sits in a wheely, red, cushioned chair, a boxy, 1960's relic shaped like Captain Kirk's throne on the Enterprise.

All our lab technicians are highly organized people who radiate a vibe of competence, though maybe that vibe is attached to the position more than to the person. I can say very little about the legendary techs from before my time. I've only heard a few stories, like the time a tech was arrested on drug charges, and while the feds were in the lab to take her away, jingling their handcuffs menacingly, she insisted they sit in the histo room and wait for three hours while she finished running behavioral tests on her monkeys.

In my own time, Nina is our longest-running tech. She gave me a present, a plastic cicada that makes a loud bug noise when you squeeze it. Helen is always dear to my heart—lovely and sunny and sparky and strong-willed. Anne is a packrat for office supplies, and her massive stash of pens and paper clips remains as a kind of monument for years after she's gone. Shafali sometimes sports henna decorations curling over her elegant brown hands. Julia likes to play with the dry ice. Su Liu has a soft spot for Q-Tip, the baby monkey. Nancy has a white plastic novelty pen in the shape of a femur—and, with a straight face and woebegone eyes, she explains to us that when she was a baby, she had her femur removed because of a disease and had it fashioned into a pen as a keepsake. When asked how she still has a functioning leg, she explains that the doctors put in a metal bone. When asked how her leg was able to grow to a normal adult size, she explains that when she was growing up, every year, the doctors had to surgically remove the previous metal bone and replace it with a new, slightly larger one. And when asked about the absence of any obvious scar on her leg, she claims that the doctors performed the surgery laparoscopically through an incision hidden under her toenail. The story grows more bizarre and lovely with each telling.

The histology room is busy, thriving, full of gleaming, organized stocks of lab chemicals and glassware, as well as equipment manuals and binders of instructions for every procedure. Three rectangular, fluorescent lights, each about a yard long and a third as much wide, are fixed to the ceiling at regular intervals like rungs of a ladder down the length of the long room. If you want to perform delicate work that requires bright light and detailed vision, such as mounting brain tissue onto glass slides, or repairing a rip in your trousers with needle and thread after you kick too high to impress your friends, you will find no better place in the lab except possibly the surgery room, where you can bring to bear the focused spotlight of a surgical lamp.

The histology room is dominated by two countertops, one running along the wall to your left as you stand in the doorway looking in, the other along the wall to your right. The countertop to the left is taller, a work surface at which you can stand while mixing chemicals or washing glassware in the big double sink. It's black, a stone counter, stained by years of chemical potions. Above it and beneath it are blue metal cabinets filled with chemical supplies and glassware. The other counter, running along the opposite side of the room, is lower, a bench at which you can sit comfortably with your feet tucked beneath. The surface of the bench is also black but is neatly covered in sheets of white, thick, waterproof paper. The paper is taped down at the edges with aqua-colored tape, lifting up in places where its glue has dried. As you look in the door, the room gives the impression of a gleaming white stripe to your right, a jet-black stripe to your left, and a white refrigerator at the far end, with an orange label on it that says, "For specimens only—no food!"

Nina tells me a story. In a distant lab, a mythical lab tech turned on an autoclave, a device that sterilizes items in a powerfully pressurized steam chamber. The metal door failed, blew like a cannon, and went through the man's chest. They found him without a rib cage, along with a bloody, two-foot-wide hole in the concrete wall behind him. That, right there, is a lab ghost story. It isn't true but does its job. I'm profoundly respectful of our autoclave. We have a portable model sitting on the black, left-hand counter in the histology room. It's heavy enough to make you go "Omph" if you pick it up to move it. It's made of steel, the sides painted off-white, the front black, with a shiny circular steel door that closes like a bank vault. It looks like a stubby tabletop cannon. It's so small on the inside that it could barely fit a bread loaf. You have to pack your surgical instruments efficiently to get a bundle into the autoclave.

I've gotten good at wrapping up my surgical instruments in brown postal paper or green cotton cloth and taping the package closed neatly with autoclave tape, like a Christmas present. I slide the package into the round torpedo tube, close the door, turn the elaborate locking mechanism, and, thanks to Nina, every time, an image rises into my head, a picture of the door blasting off and shooting out at hypersonic speeds. Our countertop autoclave is aimed more at my guts than my chest, so I'd go down in lab mythology as the guy who lost his bowels. It hasn't happened yet, but you never know.

Further down the black stone counter, past the autoclave, a fume hood hunkers near the back of the room, like a large gray beast crouching. You can just see, in the few inches of dusty space between it and the ceiling, an air duct covered in thick insulation and taped all around in silvery duct tape. A dial mounted to the dull metal side of the hood shows a twitching needle and proves that the airflow is operational. The needle looks a little like a dragonfly whose wings are constantly flickering. The idea is, when you work with chemicals that can kill you, and we often do, you should put them inside the hood, if you remember.

We use it mainly for staining tissue slides, turning brain slices into beautiful colored tendrils and spots. We populate the space inside the hood with rows of little, square, glass containers, each filled with its own magic solution in which to dip the tissue. A small metal rack holds a row of twenty specimen slides and fits neatly into the glass dipping containers. You pass it through one container after the next in the prescribed sequence, three minutes in this one, two minutes in the next, rinsed briefly in the next, seven minutes in the next. If you hear the beeping of the lab timer every few minutes, then you know someone is in the histology room, staining tissue. It's always a messy business. Some of the glass containers are filled with acetone— the terrible-smelling component of nail polish remover. Some are filled with xylene. You don't want xylene to leak through holes in your gloves because it will soak into your skin and probably give you cancer eventually. One glass container is filled with a thick, viscous, royal-purple goop, the Cresyl Violet stain, the vital substance of the histology room. It's what gives the slices of brain tissue their eventual, beautiful, purple color, and renders individual neurons visible under a microscope. It also permanently stains lab coats and street clothes.

Once, Noah, the sex-drugs guy, asked what would happen if you filled a bathtub with Cresyl Violet and submerged yourself. We were worried he might try. We called him the sex-drugs guy because he was constantly canvassing people on whether they liked sex or drugs better. He couldn't decide, himself, though we had a suspicion he had tried neither.

To the right of the fume hood is a slot, about two inches wide, between the metal wall of the hood and the concrete wall of the room. It's a secret, hidden place, a pigeon hole for those who know about it. You can slide a pamphlet of instructions in it, or a favorite pencil that you don't want anyone else to find and steal, or maybe the electronic timer, much stained with spots of Cresyl Violet. You don't want to stick your arm too far in that space, however, because it's profoundly dirty, having never been cleaned. Once, I found a large, black, leather, artist-portfolio case in that slot, tied closed at the top with black string. Surprised to see anything so unusual in that secret compartment, and curious, I slid it out, untied it, and snuck a peek at what was inside. I recognized the drawings right away—a series of charcoal sketches I had once made for a friend of mine, a lab mate. The drawings showed the two of us fucking in various positions. That sounds creepier, and more litigiously actionable, than it really was. At the time I gave them to her, the drawings were merely artistic renditions of our ordinary life together. By the time she left that portfolio in the slot, we were no longer dating. I don't know why she left them in the lab next to the histology hood. Was she trying to give them back to me? Was she attempting to send a message? Did she stick them there and forget, wondering where she had misplaced them? Puzzled and in some emotional turmoil, I left the sketches there, and after about a month the case disappeared. A tense, confusing situation, emblematic of the entire relationship. Lab romances can be tricky.

Four or five of us are sitting around the histo room in mismatched chairs, idly swiveling in our seats, talking casually, when Charlie comes stumping in with a look of purpose. He jabs a finger at the refrigerator, stares at each of us in turn with intensity, his bushy hair vibrating from his sudden movements, and blurts out, almost as though on the edge of panic, "Is Yoda in there?" Except he pronounces it as "Yoder" in his heavy Brooklyn accent. Without waiting for an answer, or opening the door of the refrigerator to check, he turns around and stumps back out.

None of us knows what he's talking about. Did we have a monkey named Yoda? Did he and Liz misplace a crucial specimen from their experiment? Why would Yoda be in a refrigerator? As his footsteps are fading down the hall, Tirin mutters, in a creaky voice, "Cold, I be."

Do you know those moments of mass, uncontrollable laughter? Eventually I study laughter and its uncanny resemblance to a defensive cringe. You bend forward with your arms crossed over your stomach, your shoulders pulled up around your neck, your knees bent, your waist bent, the skin around your eyes crinkled in spasms, your cheek flesh bunched up hard toward the eyes, tears coming out. You can't easily breathe and your diaphragm hurts. We're caught in that reflex. We can't stop ourselves.

Charlie must hear us from down the hall and I doubt he appreciates the laughter—it sounds too much like we're making fun of his goofy manner. I've never seen him laugh at other people or mock them, ever, maybe because he grew up with a stutter and a clumsy body language that was the target of too much ridicule. If he doesn't like someone, he just says so, sometimes with a shocking bluntness to the person's face. But he doesn't laugh at people. Occasionally he makes self-deprecating comments, subtly laughing at himself, but his sense of humor generally lacks cruelty. When he laughs, it's because he has a well-developed appreciation for irony. I know we shouldn't be laughing, but, "Cold, I be," is too much for us.

I feel I need to explain a contradiction. We care for the monkeys—it's our responsibility to keep them healthy and happy, and we put our hearts into the job. The experiments are

as respectful as we can make them. But at the same time, I've
told you about slicing a brain into tissue sections and possibly
even putting Yoda in the refrigerator. Here is the truth. For the
first many years of the lab, to study the brain, you would study
a monkey, measure its behavior, listen to its neurons, collect
data, and finally, after a year or so, you would sacrifice the
animal and turn its brain into glass microscope slides. What
else can I say? That's what happened.

As technology improved, it became possible to look into
the head with MRI machines. We could collect data from a
monkey, then give him a scan and have everything science
needed without sacrificing the animal. I came into the lab more
or less at that transition time. My monkeys were some of the
first to be put through the MRI machine. When I eventually
switched from studying monkeys to studying humans, I made
sure to send my monkeys to a retirement colony in Texas, where
they live in a big, raucous group under the supervision of a vet.
I believe they lounge in hammocks, sipping banana daiquiris
and reading *Tarzan of the Apes*.

I apologize for the next story. I think it's apocryphal. It dates
from before my time and smacks of a myth, another ghost story,
like the autoclave that blew out the man's chest. I'm pretty sure
it's made up. Once upon a time, in a long-ago past, hidden
in the low blue metal cabinet under the hood in the histology
room, next to the large plastic and glass containers of alcohol,
bleach, and Cetylcide Disinfectant, there was a huge, white,
ten-gallon plastic bucket filled with formaldehyde solution. It
was heavy and hard to move. If you strained and took it out
of the cabinet, put it on the floor, and pried open the plastic
cover with a screwdriver, you'd see a brown, opaque, dirty fluid
sloshing inside, with bits of fur and gray tissue floating on the
surface. The stench coming out of it was sickening. If you put
on a glove, one of those elbow-length, rubberized, dishwashing
gloves, stuck your hand in, and stirred up the fluid, you'd see
monkey heads rolling up to the surface, their half-opened eyes
translucent and wrinkled, staring blankly, until each head
rolled slowly over and disappeared again into the depths of
the liquid. To break in a new technician and make sure she had
the stomach for the job, as a first task, she'd be told, "See that
bucket? Drain out the fluid, rinse off the heads, and fill it with
fresh solution." If she survived that first task without throwing

up or running out of the lab screaming, she'd be good for the job. Happy Halloween.

At the back of the room, on top of the refrigerator, we have a ratty old cardboard box that contains our first-aid kit, our emergency protocol in a plastic binder, and our bite-and-scratch log. If you need a bandage, you'll find it here. If you need anything serious—like stitches, or forceps to remove a splinter—you'd better go to the surgery room and fix yourself properly with the vet supplies.

If you do get scratched or bitten by a monkey, there's a risk you'll catch monkey herpes, which is fatal to humans. Almost every person who has ever caught it—which amounts to extremely few, about thirty in the entire known history of the world—has died. You're supposed to log the scratch, walk across campus to the health center, get your blood drawn for testing, and begin a course of heavy antiviral medication that can cause permanent harm to your hearing and your liver. We did a back-of-the-paper-towel calculation once and realized that if a monkey were infected with that virus, bit you, and injected the virus directly into your bloodstream, your chance of getting the disease would still be microscopically less than your chance of getting killed by a car on your way across the street to the health center. Hence, for all the literally hundreds, possibly thousands, of times I'm scratched, bitten, stabbed accidentally by dirty needles, or cut by a scalpel dripping with monkey blood, or the times monkey drool has gotten on my hands and into my sandwich like a garnish, I've never once filled out the bite-and-scratch log and never taken the antiviral medication. Ethically, I can't tell anyone else what to do. But given the information available, I have my own approach. *Shhh*—don't tell anyone.

The right-hand wall of the room, as you look in the door, has a long, low workbench, resting on sturdy legs. I've mentioned it before. The surface is covered in large sheets of shiny, non-absorbent white paper taped together at the seams with turquoise tape. I think the tape was someone's attempt to match the aqua color of the metal casings in the room. The work surface is usually mostly empty, cleared and spotless. A clean workspace is a reflection of the organized mind, and our lab technicians are organized people. In Figure 1, it's labeled "Microtome." It's the place where we slice tissue samples and mount them onto glass slides.

The sliding-block microtome, sitting on the far end of the workbench near the back wall, is one of the most elegant machines in the lab. It's old, an antique that can never break or lose its value, a marvel of efficiency and precision machinery. The assemblage is mounted on a varnished, inch-thick, hard-wood board, its varnish flaking off where cold and damp has taken effect over the decades. The machine, bolted to the top of the board, is essentially a sliding track for an extremely sharp blade. The blade, polished to a mirror surface and about the size and shape of a cooking cleaver, is bolted horizontally to a block of steel, and you slide the block forward and backward noiselessly on the well-oiled track. When you slide it forward, gently and smoothly toward your chest, the blade passes over a tissue sample, a little plum-sized brain, that has been frozen with ground-up bits of dry ice packed around it. A tiny bit of tissue is skimmed off by the blade.

You take a wet paint brush, a small one with just a few hairs, wipe the clump of tissue off the blade, and drop it in a petri dish of fluid. There, the little wet rag of tissue spreads into a gossamer, beautiful section of brain, undulating like a jellyfish, white and beige, barely visible.

Then you gently push the knife away from you. It slides with a whisper back over the tissue sample. When it reaches the back end of the track, it hits a switch, the machinery clicks, and the blade is lowered by the turn of a steel screw, until it has dropped a precisely calibrated distance in preparation for its next forward cut. You can cut in increments as fine as fifteen microns, though I prefer forty or even a chunky sixty. It's a deli slicer, is what I'm saying, designed for the thinnest lunch meat possible.

I find the long process of cutting a monkey brain on the microtome to be meditative. The sound is rhythmical—the quiet icy scrape of the blade as it cuts, the metallic snick as it lowers. Your arms move cyclically like a rower's, forward and back. Your eyes are fixed on the white frozen brain tissue and on each new crumpled flower of a slice. The delicate but pervasive smell of the phosphate buffer, the slightly salty liquid into which you gently place the sections, fills up the space around you. Underneath the smell of the buffer is a bouquet of formaldehyde.

To cut an entire brain, maybe eight hundred sections, can take a day. I like to cut alone because of the sense of sequestered peace. Other people, being more sociable, tend to organize cutting parties. Sometimes the radio is on; sometimes people chat. It's a day-long event, like a barn raising. One person cuts. Two or three line up in chairs along the workbench, using paint brushes to gently coax the floating tissue sections onto glass slides. The slides are set out on paper towels to dry, and will eventually be dipped in tissue stains and studied under a microscope or drawn on the enlarger.

Charlie never participates in cutting parties because his hands aren't coordinated enough. He leaves it to the rest of us, and the social atmosphere adjusts without him, becomes a little more mainstream, a little less centered on his outlandish stories. You find out real grit about people's personal lives because, over the long hours, you run out of trivia and begin to dip into the truth. You learn about people's childhoods, their frustrations and loves and fetishes. Someone is voted to bring back sandwiches and sodas from Cox's deli. A brain party happens only a few times a year and has a festive quality, like neuroscience Christmas.

Above the workbench, running along the wall, a set of blue-green metal shelves hangs over your head. We have three shelves, one above the other, filled with about five hundred bottles of powdered chemicals in alphabetical order—some plastic bottles, some glass, a few metal canisters, colorful labels, all gleaming under the bright fluorescent lights. Each bottle remains forever, after the project that required its purchase, because nobody is sure how to safely dispose of it. Over the years, the number of bottles slowly increases. One bottle says "Cyanide." Just straight-up "Cyanide." It's used for certain kinds of tissue stains.

The lab manuals are lined up at one end of the shelves. We have half a dozen plastic binders full of stained, ripped, wrinkled pages, some typed on manual typewriters, others handwritten. They're lists, procedures, and alchemical potion recipes, like you might expect to find in an old magician's book. Pandya's stain. Nauta's silver degeneration method. Golgi's procedure. Paracelsus's mixture. Anaxagoras's prescription. Imhotep's broth. I'm making up some of these names. Anyway, they are ancient recipes. I don't even recognize most of the handwriting. It's possible that some of the pages are photocopies of documents from before Charlie was even born. Here and there I recognize Charlie's crooked block letters or Hillary's flowing script. A chunk of material is filled up with my own protocols in my stubby, block handwriting. Fifty items to check before a surgery. The exact order of procedures for an anesthetized prep. How to stitch up an injured tail, with ink illustrations. I tend toward disorganization, but I've learned how to reach inside myself, find a hidden neurotic kernel, and use it when necessary. Lists are like scaffolding to support the next experiment. I've become the most list-happy person in the lab.

A ratty old cardboard box, little noticed, never used, sits in an upper corner of the shelves. It's filled up with white plaster casts of brains. Each plaster brain has a number neatly written in black marker. I don't know why we have these casts or who made them. There must be thirty of them, at least. Are they the fruit of some forgotten procedure in the before-times? Did Charlie save them from an even more ancient lab, maybe at Harvard or MIT, where he used to work? Why would you ever want a box of plaster brains?

If you ask Charlie why we have them, he won't answer. The topic won't keep his attention. He'll shrug and mutter, "Oh, I don't know, I guess we . . . you know . . . um . . . How's your experiment?" He's not usually interested in the past. He's focused on the present and the future. If he does get onto the subject of the lab's past, he's likely to groan suddenly and say, touching his head with his hands, "Oh God, you people don't do any work. You wouldn't believe how hard we worked in the old days. You'd think I was making up a story. We lived in the lab. We ate here and slept here and had romances here, and all anyone could think about was the experiments and the data, and we worked all the time and abandoned our families like proper scientists. Now, everyone thinks they have a life. I don't understand it. They get fuck-all done. How can you expect to be a scientist and have a life outside the lab? Forty hours a week—it's a scandal! Eighty hours? It's outrageous! Tell me when you're at two hundred hours!" He'll shake his head and walk out of the room, still muttering. All this from a guy who left his lab for months at a time to hitchhike across India and China. Not to mention, there aren't two hundred hours in a week. You have to interpret everything Charlie says through the lens of caricature, and then you'll arrive at the truth he's trying to convey.

13

THE SURGERY ROOM

Michael, Michael," Charlie says. "Come help me with something." He leads me to the surgery room. "Look, I got blisters on my feet from jogging. I need you to cut them open with a number eleven scalpel." It's exactly as disgusting as it sounds.

The surgery room is a tale of old and new—the comfortable, durable old, and the cheap, glitzy new. The old surgery space was a single large room. It had the same tan linoleum floor tiles, big off-white ceiling tiles, and beige cinderblock walls as every other room in the lab. The beige was the color of a sectioned brain, with a few stray brown bloodspots that had escaped the post-surgical cleanings. The room had no sink. To scrub your hands for surgery, you had to use the sink in the histology room or the prep room, then walk down the hall with your hands held up in the air, dripping, and someone had to open the surgery door for you. We always wore proper green surgical gowns tied in back by an assistant, blue paper surgical masks, blue paper caps, and, stretched on over our scrubbed hands, long sterile latex gloves pulled over the cuffs of the gowns. We looked like real surgeons.

A white countertop ran along the east wall of the room. Under it, a set of blue metal drawers. Over it, a set of blue glass-and-metal cabinets. The drawers and cabinets were crammed with surgical supplies and instruments, sutures in little colored cardboard boxes, scalpel blades, cotton swabs, surgical sponges, IV tubing, spare gas regulators, stereotaxic frames, electric shavers, nylon strapping for monkey collars, implant gadgets, old tarnished metal head gear, plastic bottles of dental acrylic, all of it in organized chaos, like something organic, like colorful berries growing on a bush.

On the counter we always had a round metal basin, painted white, the paint chipping at the edges, filled with disinfectant solution so we could dump stray instruments in it if we needed them. Usually a long, coiled rubber hose for suction.

In the center of the room we had a surgery table made of cheap wood, wrapped over the top and sides in a thin layer of shiny tin. It was a large table, a good six feet long and three feet wide, large enough to lie down on and take a nap if you felt like it. Above the table, an enormous, old, silvery surgical lamp hung from the ceiling. I don't know where Charlie found it—hospital surplus maybe. He had a knack for scrounging free supplies. Hinged on two jointed arm segments, the lamp was obviously far too big for the room, barely maneuverable in the space available. A shiny satellite dish collimated the light downward, focusing it so brightly that when there was no patient on the table and the reflection flared back up off the metal tabletop, the light would hurt your eyes. Around the table we usually had two or three lab stools, tall steel skeletons with padded, sky-blue, vinyl seats.

To set up for surgery, we'd wheel the old Korean War anesthesia machine from the prep room down the hall to the surgery room and hook it up to the two tall air tanks, a green one for oxygen and a blue one for nitrous oxide, chained in the corner. The concrete wall there had green and blue bits of paint and streaks of rust scraped onto it from the tanks.

We'd sterilize the instruments and the surgical drape in tidy little packages in our autoclave and set them out in a row on the counter, like loaves of bread cooling down in a bakery. The surgical drape was an old brown bedsheet that Charlie donated from his house because it was too worn out to sleep on anymore. The fenestration, or the hole through which the patient's critical body part showed, was a five-inch tear in the fabric, blood-stained threads dangling off the edges. Hillary, the lab's expert seamstress, bought a sturdy cotton bedsheet in blue, cut a neat hole at one end, and stitched a hem around the hole. It was our best surgical drape for at least three months, until the hole frayed and collected bloodstains and clumps of dental acrylic. Then it was pretty much the same bedraggled mess as the old brown one.

Charlie taught me how to do surgery. First, he'd take the autoclaved package of instruments, tear it open, and dump it onto a large, metal tray, scrambling the instruments with his stubby fingers like he was mixing a salad. He always seemed to find what he was looking for better in a pile of chaos. Then he'd start pointing and explaining. He was an exceptionally patient teacher, watching me perform while he cheerfully dispensed wisdom and talked about food. In moments like these he was never critical—always lavishly positive.

I love surgery. I don't know why. It shouldn't be so fun. What does it say about me? The monkey is anesthetized, prepared, his head shaved, smooth to the skin, washed in purple Betadine soap that kills germs with its heavy component of iodine. He's put securely in a stereotaxic head holder on the table. He looks absurdly small, the size of a stuffed teddy bear on a person-sized operating surface. The heart monitor is clipped on, the temperature probe is gently inserted anally and taped to the tail to keep it in place, a warm-water pad is slid under him, and the surgical drape is spread over the table. Now the monkey is invisible, no longer a being, reduced to a small mounded circle of skin only a few inches across, an operating field under such an intense beam of light that I can see every pore, all the intricacies of the texture of the skin. I can hear the steady beeping of his heart. The lab tech sits on a stool, watching closely, writing down the vital signs.

Surgery brings me closer to the secret of life. This, in front of me, is the vital substance. I can study all its intricate layers: the skin is much thicker and tougher than it looks on the outside, beneath it a thin translucent fascia covers the muscles, and beneath the muscles a gossamer periosteum covers the bone. You cut as little as you can, always dissecting along the natural lines of separation. To steady your hands, you brace one on a hard surface—perhaps the corner of the metal stereotax frame—you brace your other hand against the first one, and by applying force in both directions, pushing your hands together with a gentle pressure, the double-ended system gives you superhuman control.

A monkey has great big packs of muscle on his head for attack biting. Charlie always says that they remind him of roast beef, and after surgery he wants to get a roast beef sandwich for lunch. We have to push the muscle aside, clear an area of bone, clean it until it's white and dry, and place the implant. As I said before, the procedure is borrowed from human surgery, when an implant is needed to monitor the brain of an epileptic patient. Sometimes we drill a little burr hole through the skull to allow a more direct access to the brain. You have to drill carefully with a high-speed dental drill, dribbling saline on the tiny steel drill bit to avoid overheating the tissue. Often, one person dribbles and sucks away the excess through the aspiration tube, while the other drills. The skull can be a quarter-inch thick in places. We put small-gauge titanium bone screws into the skull, seal the surface of the bone in dental varnish, and then build up a platform of pink dental acrylic that oozes around the heads of the screws, dries, and forms a hard, durable top. When all is done, a little, pink, hard, acrylic cap emerges from the skull, sculpted expertly, containing whatever gear we need for the next phase of the experiment, such as a small metal jar top for accessing and measuring the brain. The skin is neatly sewed up around the edges of the cap, and the surgery is over. The monkey is ready to recover, with strong painkillers, for the next few weeks. Taking off my bloody gloves, my paper hat and mask, feeling my sweaty face, reaching behind my back and pulling open the ties to the surgical gown, standing straight after bending over the surgery table, that moment, that feeling of release, is the feeling of a long, mentally intense job that's been done correctly and is over.

And yet surgery is emotionally paradoxical. For all the sense of accomplishment, of chaos tamed by my own focused attention, and of connection to the secret inner clay of which living bodies are made, at the same time, here is an animal that no longer has fur or skin on the top of his head. He's altered. He's sewn together. Have I done something horrible and wrong? I'm sorry, monkey. I'm truly sorry. The two kinds of feelings are counterbalanced. That's what surgery always is. It's physically, mentally, and emotionally exhausting. I need to sit in my office and let the surgical vapors dissipate for a while. But in the background of my mind, I never doubt the value of the science.

After a surgical procedure, or so I'm told, a monkey once woke up sooner than expected, leaped off the table, and fell into a bucket of spicy buffalo wings that the surgeons had brought in for their dinner afterward. I don't know if the surgeons picked the monkey hair off the wings and ate them anyway. To be honest, I'm pretty sure the story is made up. Sure, somebody might have eaten buffalo wings in the surgery room in the old days before the regulations, but who would have put the bucket on the floor under the surgery table? Something doesn't add up.

Whether the stories are completely accurate or embellished, the good old casual days are gone. The regulations have caught up to us. Apparently, in the new way, you can't have a surgical table made of wood. It isn't washable. You can't have visible cracks between the floor tiles. You can't sterilize old bed sheets as surgical drapes, and you can't eat dinner in the surgical suite. What will they think of next? You can see the new surgical suite in Figure 2.

The smell is horrible when they put in the new floor. Paul says it's the smell of epoxy, the resin that forms the base material of the gritty, continuous layer of mudge spread over the floor. The gray mudge extends up the concrete walls about three inches.

The room is cut in two. The front part is now a scrub station, a double steel sink that has foot pedals so that you don't have to touch dirty faucet handles. Mirrored cabinets stare at you from the wall above the sink. What I mean is, when you wash your hands, you're confronted by your own face. Why do we need to see ourselves while scrubbing for surgery? Are we going to fix our hair and makeup, like actors in a hospital TV show? The cabinets loom out of the wall in just the wrong way that, when I bend forward to scrub my hands in the sink, my nose bashes against the mirror. Who designed this awful space? It looks beautiful, shiny and clean to an inspector, but functionally, it stinks. I'd rather have the old surgery room.

Having scrubbed, I push through a swinging door to the inner room. Here, the walls have been painted a painful white. I liked the old beige better because it hid the blood splashes. The countertop along the wall is gleaming steel. The cabinets above the countertop are white metal, with glass sliding doors and little paper labels glued to the glass indicating where every implement belongs on the shelves. Because of the intense brightness of the lights, and the white surfaces everywhere, and the gleaming sterility and organization, and the perfect epoxy floor with no cracks or joints, and the petite new surgical lamp that fits the size of the space perfectly, when I step into the surgery room I feel like I'm stepping out of Charlie's lab into a bleak and unwelcoming future.

On the front of the cabinets, attached to one of the metal vertical supports, I've stuck a little clay head about an inch tall.

It's yellow with red bulging eyes, a great long nose, and some black fuzz stuck on as hair and a beard. It's the genie of the surgery room. It's the last holdout of chaos and individuality. The inspectors ask about it on one of their visits, and I tell them, with an earnest expression, that it's sterilized in ethylene oxide gas before every surgery, and it's an anatomical model useful as a guide to place the acrylic cap correctly during certain procedures. To understand this moment, you must first understand the truth about the culture of inspection and regulation. I learned it when I was briefly a part of it. For me to be recruited as an inspector and a rule enforcer is one of the crowning ironies of my life, and when Charlie heard I was on that committee he burst out laughing. They all know they're pedaling a paper façade; they know that only the smallest part of what they do concerns the actual pragmatics of safety and sterility. That is how an inspection team of individually intelligent adults can look at a preposterous clay face with hair and googly eyes, stuck to a cabinet in a surgery room, and collectively nod and accept it as a medical aid. They all know it isn't, but they're willing to accept it if it works on paper.

On the other hand, the inspectors, being sophisticates, sneer at the invaluable, unbreakable anesthesia machine from the Korean War. It looks old on paper, so whatever its actual condition or qualities, it must be replaced. Now we have a refrigerator-sized plastic hulk with knobs and dials and blinking lights. It constantly breaks and it does absolutely nothing that the MASH machine did not do better. We don't get rid of the old machine, of course—it stands unused in the back of the prep room. A skeleton. A relic of better times. I'm beginning to understand Charlie's refusal to throw anything out.

14

THREE LITTLE ROOMS

The hippocampus is a part of the brain. It's curvy, like a seahorse, which is how it got that name, "hippocampus" being Greek for "seahorse." It probably serves a lot of functions, but one is spatial memory—spatial maps. Birds that hide their food in stashes and retrieve it later have a large hippocampus. Humans have a pretty good-sized one, and London taxi drivers are notably well endowed in that area.

The hippocampus has been studied in rats more than in any other animal. They're especially good at spatial navigation, being creatures of intricate tunnels. If you monitor an individual neuron in a rat's hippocampus and let the rat wander through a complex web of tunnels and open spaces, that cell will latch onto a little dab of space that neuroscientists call the cell's "place field." The place field might be at one end of a particular tunnel or attached to a rat-sized patch of an open chamber. Whenever the rat stands in, or walks through, that particular little bit of the environment, the neuron will fire off signals. When the rat goes somewhere else, to any other part of the cage, the neuron will fall silent. In essence, with every burst of activity, the neuron signals, shouting to the rest of the brain, "Hey hey, we're here, in my home, my place field, in the special part of this world that I stand for." Different neurons represent different parts of space so that, as the rat moves around his cage, a series of cells becomes active, one after the next, tracking the animal's changing position in real time. In aggregate, a large set of place cells in the rat's hippocampus provides a virtual, spatial navigation map of the maze—of where the rat is, at any one time, in relation to the rest of the environment.

You may wonder, how can a network of place fields keep track of all space efficiently? A wild rat must visit so much space, so many places in a lifetime running through the sewers, that it might run out of neurons in the hippocampus, if each neuron represents a specific spot in the world. The answer is that the whole set of place fields is recycled and retrained for each new environment. If you put the rat in a new cage, the same place cells reinvent themselves, taking hold of the novel environment, seizing on the available places. More or less, as the rat grows accustomed, its place fields tell each other, "I call dibs on this new corner," or, "I want this spot under the food hopper," as they construct a map of the new home. For every tunnel system—every floor plan, you might say—to which the rat grows accustomed, its place cells quickly make it their own, seeking out their spots and niches, giving the rat an integrated understanding.

Why am I writing about place cells?

People have them too. When you walk into a new house, before your place cells have settled, the spaces are chaotic, confusing. Even if you can navigate your way to the bathroom by geometry and intellect, the corridors and rooms don't feel comfortable. They aren't filled up with an invisible, warm gel of familiarity. If you live in the house for a while, your experience changes. Each little corner, each location, develops its own feel, its own personality, connecting up to neighboring spaces until all the parts of the house fit together in an inexpressible logic. That is the maze of the lab to me.

One of the most spatially intricate parts of the lab stands next to the surgery room. There you'll find three small rooms packed into the space of one, curled together like a little nest within the larger nest of the lab. The baby room, the black hole, and Dylan's office. I'm pretty sure the space was designed, originally, as one large procedure room. Maybe it was going to be another prep room. The walls that divide the space into three smaller compartments are not the lab's usual cinderblock but cheap, thin plasterboard. Each one of those little rooms has its own story, its own personality, and consequently its own place fields.

15

THE BABY ROOM

A baby monkey should be raised by its mother, but sometimes that is impossible. The best way to determine whether a mother can cope, I have been told, is to assess whether the geotropism is positive or negative.

"The what is what?" I ask the vet. I never like jargon. "English please," I want to say, but I'm not so rude.

"Positive geotropism," our calm and patient vet, Norm, explains in his subtle Southern accent, "is indicated when the mother holds the baby right-side up. Negative geotropism is when she dangles the baby upside down."

I'm not sure such an obvious difference deserves the fancy jargon.

The baby room has a small metal alarm box fixed to the wall, just outside the door, and you must use a stubby silver key to turn the alarm on or off. When you open the blue door, flapping it inward against the wall where the doorknob comes to rest against a rubber stop, you see a tiny room, a refurbished closet. It's like a miniature version of the surgery room, with a sealed, gray, mudge floor, bright white walls, and a bright rectangular fluorescent light glaring down. A steel countertop with a sink runs along part of one wall, stopping in just the right place to allow the door to open. Above the countertop, a white metal cabinet is mounted to the wall, and is full of supplies for the babies such as infant formula and baby bottles and laundered towels. The room is so small and packed, it makes me think of an efficiency kitchen in a camper truck. Even though it looks new and glaringly bright, I don't see it as a violation of the Charlie lab aesthetic because it was built before I arrived, and so, of course, I never knew it any other way.

Crammed into the room are two upright cage racks, each about six feet tall, facing each other from opposite corners across the little space. Each rack has two cages, a lower and an upper. Each cage, at about three feet cubed, is a cathedral compared to the size of a baby monkey. A very young baby cuddled in blankets is about the size of a hamster, and an active toddler, climbing around the inside of its cage, is the size of a squirrel. We put stuffed animals in the cages for the babies to hug at night, but they tend to chew on the plastic eyes until the black pupils are gone and the toys develop a spooky, possessed look with a blank white stare. The babies like them anyway.

My primary job, my very first job when I arrive in the lab as an undergraduate in the late 1980s, is to take care of the babies. And I take my job seriously. Every day, first, I weigh each baby. I take the balance scale down from the cabinet, put it on the steel countertop, plop a baby in the little tin basin on one side and balance it against the beige plastic weights on the other side. The weights, I think, are filled with metal shot, judging by how they rattle. Three hundred grams. Five hundred grams. Seven hundred grams. The babies are very small.

Then I feed them. For the youngest ones, I mix up regular human baby formula and fill up a tiny, plastic, doll's bottle. I hold the baby in one hand, wrapped up in a fuzzy green terrycloth towel, and hold the doll bottle in the other hand. For the older babies, I soak a Purina monkey biscuit until it's soft, mash it up with some human banana baby food, and then spoon the mixture into their mouths on a tiny plastic spoon.

Here's how you give a baby monkey a bath. First, put the monkey in your open palm. It'll reflexively cling on, its little legs locked around your wrist, its arms stretched out and locked around your palm, the head pointing up toward your fingers, the long dark tail hanging down your forearm and tickling you on the inside of the elbow joint. Then you turn on the sink faucet and adjust it to a gentle, warm flow. Then you hold the monkey under the water. It snuggles as the water plashes over its fur, and it goes to sleep in the warmth. When you're done, you must dry off the monkey thoroughly with a soft towel so that it doesn't get cold. I don't know if the baths are protocol, but I like them and the monkeys love them. And they smell better afterward.

What they like most, however, is playing. I spend hours sitting on the gray floor between the two cage units, my back against the wall, soft towels draped over my crossed legs. A young baby is sleeping in my lap. An older one is skittering around the floor. Another one is climbing up the outside of a cage. The older babies are like rubber balls bouncing everywhere, their legs springing off the walls and the counter and the top of my head. I sit quietly and watch the commotion and the joyful squealing. We are a family. I can sit here for hours. In my teen manifestation in the 1980s, gaunt and tall, twiggy arms and legs, a shock of dark brown hair spreading over my shoulders, and a shaggy, uneven beard and mustache, I look like a gigantic monkey and fit right in.

16

THE BLACK HOLE

It used to be Earl's office. Then Tirin and Hillary rebuilt it as an experiment room and painted the inside a flat black, to reduce light scatter. After that, we called it the black hole. Specifically, Tirin's black hole. Eventually, Dylan and I, and The Mole (a monkey), took over and conducted a long series of experiments in there.

The room is crowded with equipment. A neurophysiology rig is a beautiful expression of chaos. An explosion of wires and clutter. As you look in the door, to your left stands the main part of the rig, the monkey's island. The monkey sits on a low table in his plastic chair, surrounded on all sides and above by equipment and wires. The Grass stimulator, one of the most visually impressive pieces of equipment ever designed, with a boxy body the size of an oven and about eight hundred dials and knobs on its front, sits on a plywood platform directly over the monkey's head. A rusty iron pipe, about an inch and a half in diameter, rises from the floor to the ceiling beside the monkey's table. It's one of the most prominent parts of the apparatus, built so solidly it looks as if it should support heavy equipment, but its only function is to support a small beaker of apple juice for the monkey.

We train The Mole to play hockey—Dylan's favorite sport. The idea is to test how the brain changes as it learns new hand-eye coordination. We make a plywood table-hockey rink about the size of a dinner tray, fashion a little white hockey puck out of a tape roll, and train The Mole to whack at it with a stick in his hand and knock it into a goal, at which achievement he receives a squirt of juice through a tube in his mouth. It's not clear if he ever fully grasps the concept. Unlike chimpanzees and humans, our monkeys are not natural tool users.

We've also tested his brain's responses to the sight of a fake arm. First, we visit a taxidermist and purchase two monkey arms, a left and a right, for $300 each. I don't know the going price for arms, but it seems expensive to me. Then, we strap The Mole's own arms into a padded holder, cover them from sight with a lid, and place the fake arms on the lid. A clever bit of arrangement, some drapery, obscures the fact that the fake arms are sawn off at the shoulder and unattached to the monkey. It looks like he's casually sitting with his arms stretched out on a table surface.

Dylan and I are so proud of our work that we call Tirin into the room. He looks, shrugs, and says, "So? What's the big deal? I don't get it."

His reaction outrages us until we realize the problem. He doesn't notice that the arms are fake. Looking closer, he says, "Your monkey is ridiculously well behaved, though. How do you get him to be so well behaved? Look, he's not moving his hands at all!"

"Yeah?" I say, "You want him to move his hands? Watch this!"

I grab one of the fake arms, pause for dramatic effect, and then yank it right off, apparently wrenching it out of the socket and waving it around the room. The monkey doesn't care. He knows it's not his arm. But Tirin screams, his eyes round for two seconds before he digests what really happened.

Those fake arm studies reveal a region of the brain that cleverly combines joint sensation with visual appearance in order to keep track of the position of one's own arms. The experiments are arduous. For several hours a day, every ten seconds, one of us must cover the monkey's eyes with a piece of cardboard, rearrange the angles of the arms, both real and fake, then uncover his eyes, before the next five-second window of data collection begins. Whoever is on arm-changing duty sits on a lab stool near the monkey, my favorite little sky-blue stool with the square seat and the four wheels at the bottom, and must meticulously consult a piece of paper listing the schedule of arm configurations, checking off one configuration after the next with a pencil. We are low tech. Low tech is always better. Another lab would have spent half a million dollars on an arm-switching apparatus, or perhaps on virtual reality.

The Mole is an important monkey to us, the star of many crucial experiments, and we include him in the acknowledgements of our papers as "T. Mole," or sometimes, "Theodore

Mole." He's egotistical, wiry, feisty, and exceptionally toothy. I never saw a monkey with such long and sharp canine teeth. We're pretty sure he has a metal file hidden in his fur. When nobody's watching, he takes it out and sharpens his canines. He's energetic and eager to get into the equipment to do the many jobs he's been trained to do, and often irritated when his testing ends for the day. That work ethic is typical of the monkeys. They grow used to the game and come to depend on it. They regard their jobs in a competitive, narcissistic manner. Theodore Mole is not a cuddly animal—I think he'd bite your jugular if you tried to hug him—but he's an ideal experimental companion. Long may he live in the Texas retirement colony, impressing the lady monkeys with his exceptional dentition.

17

DYLAN'S OFFICE

Do you know how you can naturally sense all the parts of your body? You don't need to think of each part explicitly—you don't usually notice what each joint feels like—but there's always a part of your mind, under the surface, that feels whole, that invests the full volume of your bone and flesh with a sense of being. Every finger, every toe, is part of your larger, extended consciousness. It's called the body schema, and I've spent years studying its implementation in the brain. It's also how I feel about the lab, especially at night when I'm alone and the commotion of the day doesn't distract me. It's as if my mind fills up the lab, flowing into every room and corridor. I'm not intellectually thinking my way through the rabbit warren of rooms. I just feel it, constantly with me. The extended place has been incorporated into my body schema. I feel whole, and vast, and complete, when I'm in the lab.

Sometimes, I need to get up and move around. I might venture outside the lab to the bathroom, or to the soda machine in the basement, which makes me feel vulnerable, like a snail out of its shell. Sometimes I even venture out of the building, across campus, to the all-night store, Wawa, and buy an Italian sub with hot peppers. Or maybe I'll buy some donuts. Or a chilidog. Always something unhealthy. Getting up and moving around is a good way to clear my mind and see through an idea whose subtlety is giving me trouble. But usually, the best way to sort my thoughts is to focus on something in the familiar safety of the lab itself, something mindless and repetitive, like pitching a tennis ball down the length of Corridor B. Or opening Maz's door and throwing darts at his dartboard.

First, it's just the empty vestibule outside Earl's office and the baby room. An architectural blank space. Then Tirin and

Hillary turn it into the telemetry center for the black hole,
filling it with shelves and equipment, desks and monitors. Then
Maz turns it into an office. He puts up a dartboard at the back,
fixed to the narrow west wall. When Maz is not in his office, I
can practice darts—with his permission, of course. He typically
leaves by 5:00 or 6:00 p.m., I stay until 3:00 a.m., sometimes
4:00, so I have a lot of time to improve my game.

He has three heavy, metal darts, one blue, one red, and one
purple, and after every three throws, I have to collect them and
try again. Sometimes I spend hours in a night tossing darts,
thousands of tosses, ticking off each score in ink in a data
notebook. It allows me to think. I've worked my way through
conceptual tangles and confusions as my hand and my eye settle
into a rhythm, and the dartboard has become rather ragged in
the process. It looks a terrible mess and I feel bad ruining Maz's
property. Oh, and by the way, after all that dedicated practice,
I stink. You might think I'd get good, but no such luck. I can
reliably hit the board from twelve feet away.

Maz eventually packs up and takes his dartboard with him.
Now it's Dylan's office.

Suppose you stand in Corridor B and look in the open door
of Dylan's office. To your left you'll see a set of dark brown,
wooden shelves, fixed high on the wall on black iron brackets.
The shelves are crammed full of equipment, relay boards,
eye coil drivers, an amplifier for neuron activity, a monitor
for spying on the monkey through a camera. Black wires run
everywhere, chaotically, strung across the office space. You
have to duck to get through Dylan's office or the curving wires
will catch in your mouth and around your neck.

A chain of green plastic monkeys with hook arms dangles
from the wires. Dylan and I have a proclivity for playing with
toys, so as The Mole is in the black hole playing with his table
hockey, or whatever fidget toy he has at the moment, the two of
us, Dylan and I, are sitting just outside the door, fidgeting with
the green monkeys, or a ball of orange putty, or the realistic
rubber hand.

We have a special fondness for fake hands, it seems. The
lab has a rubber human hand that looks plausibly real until
you inspect it closely and discover how pitted and grubby it is.
I've mentioned it before. Once, when Liz Gould walks past the
open door of Dylan's office on her way to meet with Charlie,

I jump out of my seat and say, "Um, Liz, can you take a look at some data?" I'm holding a sheet of graph paper in my hand.

Always helpful, she leans over to look.

My hand, holding the paper, suddenly falls out of my long-sleeved shirt and thumps on the floor. It's the rubber hand. Liz screams and jumps back about two yards. "Don't do that!" she shouts at me. "Don't do that kind of thing to me!" If I didn't know her better, I'd think she was genuinely angry. But I can see the humor lurking around her mouth. She always has that touch of sardonic humor.

Since Dylan's office doubles as the control booth for the Black Hole, at least three extra chairs are crammed into the little space for spectators. It's a crowded scientific nexus of the lab for many years. Me, Charlotte, Dylan, Xintian, Tirin, Charlie, we cycle through in twos and threes. In a fit of restlessness during an experiment, one day, I pick up a pencil and sketch an elaborate face on the wall. I don't know why. I just do.

Dylan says, "Hey, it's Charlotte!"

Charlotte bends to peer curiously.

"No, it's not!" I say, horrified. "It's not Charlotte!" I hope not, because it's hideously ugly. I don't want to offend anyone. And I shouldn't be drawing on the walls—I've defaced Dylan's office and Charlie's lab. Oops. I tend to fidget first and ask questions second. Oh well. I don't suppose anyone minds, except possibly Charlotte, who rolls her eyes and shrugs. Later, when Charlie sits down to join the experiment, his gaze passes over the drawing and then darts briefly to me—he knows who drew it—but he says nothing. Sometimes you can't tell what passes through his mind.

At the back of Dylan's office, just outside the baby room, the ceiling is gently caving in. A discolored, soggy ceiling tile has a hole cut in it about six inches in diameter, and a joint of pipe sticks through. Apparently, a water pipe in the ceiling hangs down a little too low at this location, and the simplest solution the architects could think of was to let it hang through the ceiling. The cloth and plaster insulation on the pipe, raggedy, unraveling like an old mummy, damaged by years of condensation and rust, dangles down, shreds of white wrapping slyly touching your head if you pass under that spot, as if the lab itself is conducting a secret phrenology experiment on you. We don't mind. It's a part of the scenery, a part of the eccentricity of the lab.

18

THE COLONY: HEART OF THE LAB

The purpose of the lab is to study monkeys. The living heart of the lab, therefore, is the monkeys' home space, the colony. It's a cathedral—the largest room in the lab. A vast, intimidating space. No matter how many times I walk in, I'm always impressed by the size. Never mind any low-hanging ceiling tiles—this place has a twelve-foot vault crossed by concrete beams and pipes and ventilation ducts. The floor is made of red tiles, each tile about four inches across, the dark gray grout between them unusually wide, a quarter inch. They look exactly like the floor tiles in South Station, Boston, by the way. Must be the same tile company. Go and look, if you want a clear image of the colony floor. The walls are cinderblock, not beige but white, the bright paint glossy and waterproof. The windows are blocked up. They used to be regular glass windows, looking out over the parking lot and catching the eastern sunlight, but somewhere along the way the regulators insisted we brick them in.

Very little in the colony is sound absorbent, except the monkeys. The whole place echoes. It's loud. If you scuff your shoes on the floor, the sound resonates. If you talk, you need to speak clearly or the words roll together into reverberations. As the monkeys casually grunt or hoot or rattle the sides of their cages to posture at each other, the sound echoes and amplifies. The room is under intense negative air pressure in an attempt to keep the animal stink from spreading into the rest of the lab. Because of that air pressure, when you open the door, you hear a whistle and a whoosh, and you may find it difficult to close the door again as you push against the force of the air current.

Sometimes I have monkey anxiety dreams. Turns out, comparing notes, everyone in the lab does. In one of my most common dreams, I've taken a monkey on vacation. Don't know why. Don't know how it got through airport security. But I know my solemn responsibility is to care for the animal until I can bring it back safely to the lab. Instead, the monkey gets eaten by one of the family cats. Or run over by a car. Or snatched by a hawk. The disasters are endless. Sometimes I look behind the couch and find its dusty skeleton. A sense of failed responsibility, of dread, horror, fills me and wakes me up. Once, I dreamt that a monkey's head came off and, panicking, I tried to get it back on with autoclave tape. Nothing I did worked, and the tape kept tangling and sticking to my fingers. These dreams may give you a sense of how deep-down we feel our responsibility to the animals. They depend on us in every way.

We try hard to keep them happy. Enrichment is the key. We stock their cages with toys, such as black rubber chew toys meant for dogs, or lengths of hard plastic tube filled with hidden treats that the monkeys have to winkle out. Every cage has a small, round, plastic mirror hanging from a chain. The monkeys don't generally look at themselves, but they use the mirrors to look at each other.

They even have a large TV on a wheeled cart, though I'm not convinced they watch it. It looks good on paper to regulators, but in reality, the monkeys are about as attuned to their TV as your pet dog is to yours. We used to play Animal Planet for them, until one day we heard a din of outraged screeching and yelling from the colony. We ran in and found a program on tigers in full swing. I guess the monkeys had at least half an eye on the screen and recognized the snarling face of a big cat. Since then, we've stuck to less offensive channels like the news. That's how we learn about current events—standing in a lab coat in the colony, watching TV.

Exotic food works better than TV, if you want to entertain the monkeys. Any kind of fruit or vegetable will delight them—apples and bananas will do—but we especially like to thrill them with novelty. Mangos, star fruit, kiwis, yams, watermelon, kumquats, coconuts, however expensive, we like to give it a try, not for the nutrition—which the monkeys get from their biscuits—but to offer them some excitement. Fascicularis monkeys are omnivorous in the wild. Though they mainly eat fruit, they are known to eat eggs, insects, lizards, and crabs. That's why they're commonly called crab-eating macaques. (I imagine them crowded around a table with bibs on, cracking open crab legs.) We've tried them on raw chicken eggs, which they like. We've given them snowballs in the winter, which they treat as objects of intense fascination.

During the great cicada year, when lawns and sidewalks were covered in a hundred billion large, winged bugs with bulging red eyes, and you couldn't walk across the parking lot without crunching on them at every step, we collected a bucket of cicadas and fed them to the monkeys. Al Gore especially liked them. As soon as he saw a fluttering cicada pinched in my fingers, he'd crouch down and smack his lips, eyes wide, fingers outstretched and quivering in excitement. The level of joy was beautiful. He'd grab the cicada, stuff it in his mouth and crunch it down, a wing or two sticking out.

The monkeys even go on play dates. We pair, triple, or qua-druple them for company, and every few weeks swap who vis-its who—meaning, male and female. I guess it's like a swingers club. They get along well. Some of the pairings result in babies, though we never know who the father is. Long live Ma (which, in Chinese, means horse) and Fruita (named after a town in Colorado), both born in the lab, raised with loving kindness by us humans, and now enjoying life in an open-air colony some-where in Texas.

The gray lines in Figure 1 represent caging. You can see smaller squares that represent individual cages, and a larger, encompassing rectangle that represents the outer safety enclosure. The outer enclosure is made of steel mesh with a diamond pattern. It never rusts, so I think it's galvanized. The thicker line segments along its perimeter represent mesh doors that can latch closed. This outer cage is about eight feet tall and is roofed in the same diamond mesh. If a monkey escapes it, you can be sure he'll climb up and run around on top of that mesh roof. From there, he's likely to jump up to the pipes in the ceiling. Getting him down is a long, tricky process of banana diplomacy. I've climbed up on that uncomfortable diamond-mesh roof more times than I care to admit, and scrambled around on all fours, with only four feet of clearance to the ceiling of the room. There are little bits of blackened, petrified banana permanently stuck to the mesh from past escapes.

Charlie says there are three categories of monkey. When you approach an escaped monkey, the first kind moves away from you. The second sits still. The third looms toward you. Watch out for that third kind—it has no fear of you, and with its instinct for hierarchical dominance, it might kill you. Imagine a German shepherd coming at you, but with canines roughly twice as long, and the capacity to attack from any direction in all three dimensions.

The advice is well meant, but in all the years of the lab, every monkey except for one has been well behaved. We've had pet monkeys that sit on our laps and run up and down the lab corridors. We've had nervous monkeys that scratch you if you annoy them but otherwise treat you with respect. I've been bitten many times, but only by accident when a monkey was snapping food from my hand. No monkey ever bit me with aggressive intent. We've had only one crazed, violent individual, who, when he escaped his cage, leaped on Hugo's head and bit him so hard that the two upper canine teeth punctured an inch through his plastic goggles and came within a hair's breadth of his eyeballs. When that monkey first arrived, before anyone knew about his temperament, we named him—this is true—Mahatma Gandhi. Pol Pot, part of the same batch of monkeys, was a sweetheart.

The individual cages, inside the larger enclosure, are about three feet on a side. I don't like them. They're too small. The cages are arranged in rows of four, with a lower and an upper tier, and therefore, with sixteen boxes shown in Figure 1, there are thirty-two cages. We don't have thirty-two monkeys. Usually about half of the cages are empty.

Here's the best way to get a monkey out of a cage and into a chair. The secret is a thing called love. Felix has been well trained with fruit and kindness. You wheel his plastic chair into the safety enclosure, lock the door behind you so he doesn't go anywhere inconvenient, open up the door to his home cage, and stand back. He climbs casually out, scratching himself on the ribs, pulling a half-chewed biscuit out of his mouth to inspect it and putting it back in, making faces at the other monkeys, moving bit by bit with only the most casual glance at you. With a hop, he lands on the chair and crawls in, lifts his head, and waits for you to fasten the plastic collar that keeps him in the chair. Then you hand him a reward—a piece of banana, perhaps—and wheel him out of the colony to perform his button task. Maybe you give him a scratch behind the ears, or pet him along the spine.

If you're not his familiar experimenter, you can try to chair him in the same way—wheeling in the chair, opening his cage door—but it won't work. He won't get in the chair. He'll go on a casual stroll through the colony, climb here and there, and if you talk to him and gesture at the chair, maybe with some growing desperation, he'll cast a glance over his shoulder at you that plainly says, "Piss off." You'll have no luck until you fetch his regular human partner.

Passing underneath each row of cages is a long, sloping, metal pan. The monkeys drop waste and food debris into these pans, and every half hour, on a timer, water flushes through the pans and pushes the waste out. The waste is supposed to flush into tin tubes and down into a drain in the floor. But the flush system doesn't work perfectly, and twice a day someone must go into the colony, uncoil the hose, and thoroughly spray down the pans and the whole room.

I've cleaned the colony many, many times. On weekends and on holiday, the students take turns. Some of the students hate it and would prefer to avoid it, but I find it a comforting ritual. Like pitching a tennis ball down the hall, or throwing darts, it has a mindless physicality that comforts the body and frees the mind. And I like to keep the monkeys company.

I wear a dirty white lab coat, large and loose enough that I won't feel a sweaty squeeze around my body. Also, a white disposable hair net, which will keep the larger particles off, and a white face mask, and latex gloves, but I don't wear the blue paper shoe covers because I don't want to slip and break my skull on the hard tile floor. Instead I wear old ratty sneakers. I prefer old clothes, disreputable old jeans and a T-shirt, although they don't look any different from my regular day clothes. I'm not a sharp dresser.

I unwind the hose from the casing on the wall, step into the safety enclosure, and begin to spray. The monkeys watch me with their beady brown eyes, the braver ones casually yawning at me, showing their long knife-like canines in a subtly aggressive gesture, the meeker ones turning around and presenting their butts while grinning anxiously over their shoulders.

Once all the shit and the uneaten biscuits have been hosed from the pans and down the tin tubing to the floor level, inevitably the floor drain clogs. Too many hard biscuits wedge against each other. The floor is engineered at a slant, or more like a funnel, gently easing down toward the central drain, and a massive puddle forms at that low point, spreading out perhaps fifteen feet all directions and a good three inches deep in the middle, brown and fetid, the floating biscuits slowly bloating from water absorption.

The colony room has a giant rubber squeegee, about a yard wide, attached to a long, brown, wooden broom handle. The trick is to take that squeegee, turn it around, and bash its wooden haft down a good foot into the floor drain, smashing up the biscuits lodged in there. I have to stand in the center of the lake in my sneakers. Hugo wears special green rubber boots, which makes more sense, but I personally don't like the tight sweaty feel of boots. When the biscuits are broken up, the lake suddenly drains, leaving behind a scum of debris across the floor. I use the hose and the squeegee to coax the shit and biscuit scum down the drain. I like to make sure the floor is extremely clean—it's a point of pride.

When I'm done, I'm soaked in sweat even more than in backsplash. My clothes are wet, my hair is wet, and I stink of monkey biscuit, monkey shit, and just plain natural essence of monkey. I leave the colony, peel off the protective gear, which wasn't terribly protective after all, and sit in my office chair to rest, evaporating sweat. I guess I'll go home and take a shower. If I'm feeling lazy, I might not. My office is directly next to the colony, and the air in that corridor smells like monkey anyway. If I don't mind the smell, then I'm not too concerned about how other people take it.

19

MY PERFECT OFFICE

I told you about the first office I ever had, behind the refrigerator in the lunchroom. As a teenager, I was absurdly proud of that alcove. Later, I move in with Paul into the office next to the monkey colony. When Paul leaves, Mike moves in with me.

Life is never completely calm or safe with Mike Colombo. He's both a prankster and a lightning rod.

He loves junk food and often buys a specific kind of pretzel cookie from the vending machine in the basement. One evening, I find a sealed plastic package of those cookies on his desk. He must have been saving them for the next morning, maybe dreaming about them all night. It just so happens that the lab is trying a new brand of monkey chow. Instead of the usual, roughly rectangular lumps, the pieces are shaped into little flowers about an inch across. Maybe they've been stamped out by a machine. They look a lot like small cookies. The wires in my brain connect, and I see what to do. With Xintian's help, I perform surgery on Colombo's plastic package of cookies, cutting it open with a scalpel along the line of a seam where the cut will be nearly invisible, emptying the cookies (and eating them), and replacing them with monkey biscuits. We seal up the cut with invisible tape, again cleverly hidden in the seam of the package.

The next day, Mike starts to scream. I'm not sitting in the office, but I hear him from down the hall and come running to look. He has a specific sound, a scream of shock and outrage and appreciation that transforms gradually into a long, loud laugh. He comes lurching out of the office into the corridor holding a monkey biscuit, shouting for me. "Mike! You asshole! You almost had me! I had it right up at my mouth before I smelled it!" The weak point in the plan was always the unmistakable, pungent, awful smell of monkey chow. We were never going to get him to eat the stuff.

Xintian comes scampering down the corridor from the shop room, grinning eagerly, and says, "Is he going to beat you?"

I don't get beaten, to Xintian's disappointment. Colombo is the most appreciative butt of a joke I've ever met. You have to make the joke good, however, or it doesn't even rate a laugh.

When Colombo moves to New Zealand, he leaves me a special present, his way of graciously telling me that the office is now all mine. He cuts up a porn magazine and hides the pictures around the office. "Just so you know," he says, smiling sweetly, "you'll find the easy ones right away, but don't think you're done. I guarantee you'll be finding them for years."

He's right. I search thoroughly and find about thirty pictures, awful raunchy stuff full of fetishistic fisting. It's hair-raising. Where did he even find a magazine like that? The rate of discovery slows and stops after a few days, and I hope I'm safe. But over months and years, now and then, a picture turns up.

I need more photocopies of a particular book chapter. The chapter, which Charlie and I wrote together, is published in a massive hardcover tome on my bookshelf, a yellow Post-it sticking out to mark the correct page. I hand the book to Maida, the secretary, who runs off another twenty copies as usual and brings the book back to me with a funny look in her eyes. Right away I have a suspicion, open the book to my chapter, and find a horrid picture of double fisting staring back at me. So I have to apologize and explain to Maida what happened, and that I would never plant a picture on purpose to shock her. She understands. She's very kind about it. But I'm curious why she didn't say anything. Evidently, she carefully put the picture back in the book when she was done photocopying.

Two years later, Sandy, the lovely, soft-spoken computer tech, visits my office to fix my desktop computer, opens the casing, and finds a full-page nasty porn picture on the motherboard. Sandy is intensely religious, a born-again Christian, and I'm grabbing my hair and thinking, *oh crap! Colombo!* I explain the prank to her. She's nice about it and thanks me for the explanation, although she doesn't seem to find the prank amusing or the explanation compelling. She shrugs, nods, and says, "I just thought that's where you keep your porn, Mike."

Lina, the funny and innocent undergraduate who works with me on the auditory study, is lounging in my office in the extra chair, casually chatting. She sees a blue postal tube dangling from the wall, tied by a length of string to a screw, and asks me about it. "That's my diploma," I explain. "You have to hang your diploma on the wall, right? So . . . there it is."

With a laugh, she takes it down and opens the tin end to look inside. She wants to see what a Princeton PhD diploma looks like. Instead, unrolling it, she gets an eyeful of fetish porn. "Found another one, Mike," she calls out, giggling and handing it to me.

Slowly, over years, the porn disappears, the office becomes mine—I grow into it.

By now, I've done so many experiments that the log books occupy an entire shelf on the bookcase. Some are black-bound sketch books, some are green-bound ledger books, one is an artisanal book with a red-and-pink, faux-marble pattern on the cover, bought at a store in Woodstock when the lab was visiting Charlie's house there. Sometimes, to impress people with my crazed dedication, I pull down a data book and flip open to an entry dated from Christmas day. Every Christmas, as I am always happy to brag about, I run an experiment. Everyone else may be home celebrating, but I'm in the lab collecting data. That's like genius-level obsession, right there. The Christmas entries are proof. I don't usually mention that my family celebrates Christmas a week late, to avoid the traffic and crowds, so it's really all the same for me as for anyone else.

Pasted onto the metal side of the bookshelf, you'll see a crooked sticker from the World Wildlife Foundation with a picture of a panda. Under it, a Greenpeace sticker and a Save the Whales sticker. Seamus put them there when the bookshelf belonged to him. I don't mind the stickers and leave them where they are. It may seem odd to combine lab animal research with animal activism, but pretty much everyone in the lab is strong on both interests. Maybe it explains why we try so hard to take care of our monkeys and why, in the end, we send them to retirement colonies.

Beyond the bookcase, you'll see a corkboard with a wooden frame, just to the right of my desk, filled with memoranda. Addresses, phone numbers, to-do lists. I have a postcard from Betsy from her travels in Istanbul, addressed, "Merhaba, M."

I have a piece of lined paper with Shalani's parents' address written in her neat cursive, in case I need to contact her on vacation. I have a picture of a woodchuck that Mary gave to me. I have a postcard from Dylan showing the tower of Pisa collapsing because a monkey has jumped on it (the monkey is labeled "The Mole"). I have a fragment of a leaf, now brown, that I took from my family's farm and brought to the lab to remind me of the wild, outdoor places where I grew up.

My office window, just behind the desk, is always closed and covered by venetian blinds. The blinds are white metal, dusty from disuse, and absolutely never raised or rotated from the most extreme closed position. I don't like direct sunlight. I'm comfortable only in an enclosed, hidden lair. A mellow glow of sunlight filters around the edges of the window shade, and that's all the natural light I can stand. Usually the massive, rectangular fluorescent light in the ceiling keeps the office harshly bright.

A white shoelace dangles from the ceiling over my desk. The top end is caught around one of the white metal runners on which the ceiling panels rest. The bottom end hangs within two feet of the surface of the desk, tied to the leg of a small wooden monkey. The monkey is bungee jumping, you see, dangling upside down. When our lab tech, Anne, was leaving and cleaning out her desk, I asked if I could keep her little wooden monkey, and she kindly let me.

The room contains three tall metal file cabinets, crammed in. My own and Charlie's files have intermingled, almost like the once-separate belongings of a married couple. Sometimes he stands in my office rifling through my file drawers. Sometimes I stand in his office, rifling through his.

My special chair has changed over the years, but the one I like best is a green scoop, plush, with five spoke-like, wheeled legs. I like it for its ergonomic design. It allows me to sit extremely low to the ground and lean back so that I'm nearly horizontal while working at my computer. The wheels don't move well on the linoleum tiles. They've scraped the tiles so badly that the space in front of my desk is a chaos of black and gray specks and gouges, and makes a gritty sound when you walk on it. It looks like an animal has been gnawing at it. Even the janitor can't fix it.

The room is mostly undecorated, a hoarder's collection of books and equipment, stacks of reprints and old tatty jackets on the extra chairs, but I've hung one framed photo on the wall. Charlie took the photo in India. It's a shockingly orange monkey, a *Macaca mulatta*, sitting on a carved stone god in a ruined temple, holding a half-eaten piece of fruit. I like the picture. I found it cast aside in the shop, unwanted, and took it for myself.

I think this is the best office I'll ever have. It's not luxurious and definitely does not project status. It's tiny and hidden, spartan, dirty, locked away, private and yet surrounded by a lab family. My door is never closed during the day because the lab itself has a secure perimeter. I can meet and talk to anyone from the outside, but only by invitation and appointment. No strangers can drop in on me. My back is to the door, a vulnerability I would normally find intolerable, but in Charlie's lab I don't mind. People go up and down the corridor behind me. Cages rattle past, people wheel their monkeys past, and every time the colony door opens I hear a wash of sound, the rushing noise of the ventilation system and echoing monkey calls, and then the door bangs closed and the sounds are muffled. If I don't have those constant interruptions pulling on me, like sand bags off the side of a balloon, I can't control my wandering mind. My imagination drifts away and leaves reality all together. I need the distractions to get any work done.

I hope this office is mine for eternity. I wonder if such a thing is possible? If there could be a universe of eternal temporal stasis, would I park myself here, in this green chair at my desk? Either here, I think, or in one of the experiment rooms hunting for neurons. And I would park everyone else in their places around me, like perpetual heavenly bodies, the monkeys hooting and happily eating their fruit of the day in the colony room, the students and techs talking and roaming around the spaces of the lab, and Charlie in his office, now and then coughing asthmatically or calling out to us to come help him with one thing or another. I guess writing this book is a version of that eternal stasis.

20

MAIDA'S OFFICE

To reach Charlie's office, you must pass through the secretary's space. I call it Maida's office, because she worked here longer than any of our other secretaries. It's a little space, really just a vestibule to the larger office beyond. It's big enough for two small desks, a black wooden cart for the shared printer, and a metal stand for the electric typewriter. The space always smells like ground-up pencil. An old-fashioned pencil sharpener, the kind that you turn with a crank handle, hangs from the bottom side of a wooden shelf. Charlie prefers pencils. I've seen him many times cranking away at the sharpener with a spastic energy, and I wonder how he can get the pencil sharpened without shattering it.

The walls of Maida's office are lined with long, white, wooden shelves, fixed to the wall on shiny steel brackets. The shelves are filled with rows of cardboard boxes, some brown and some green, containing copies of Charlie's published papers. His entire career is spread out, year by year. The amount of material is staggering and a little demoralizing to me. On the front of each box a label has been pasted. Maida typed them. Neat labels are not entirely possible on a typewriter— the letters are slightly uneven in tone and position, just enough to give an impression of raggedness that was probably not noticeable before the age of laser printers. It looks quaint to a more modern eye. Many of the labels have corrections in whiteout, which is even more quaint.

On a bit of free wall space next to the window, Charlie has hung some enlarged photos of his trip to Papua New Guinea. One shows an old tribesman in profile, sporting a massive gray beard, feathers in his hair, skin painted, grinning, face-to-face with Charlie, who sports his own grin and massive gray beard.

The blue-green, wooden door to Charlie's office, next to Maida's desk, is almost always swung wide open. It sports a large poster encased in a clear plastic sheath, fixed on with thumbtacks around the edge, nearly covering the entire door. The poster looks old, yellowed or brownish, and contains an elaborate, black ink drawing of a Hindu god with a devilish face, sitting on a carven throne, grimacing horribly, and having sex with a much smaller woman, who is perched on his lap, her back to the viewer, her head twisted around so that you can see her sharpened teeth and inhuman face. The drawing is stylized and filled with swirls and action and testicles. That image is your introduction to Charlie's office.

21

CHARLIE'S OFFICE: SOUL OF THE LAB

The emotional, scientific, ethical, idiosyncratic, and inspirational energy of the lab emanates from Charlie's office. In writing this account, I'm discovering the frustrating impossibility of putting *every* detail from my memory onto the page. I've captured at best 10%. But I want to put extra effort into Charlie's office. It's the soul of the lab because Charlie is the soul of the lab. I want you to know what it's like to walk in here, stand in the center of the room and look around, see, hear, smell, breathe, feel the carpet under your feet, sit down as a guest. Maybe, if I try hard, I can capture one of our lab meetings. Just that—just a moment in time, sitting in a cozy group of seven or eight people, crowded together in one bubble of personal space, talking, laughing, arguing, occasionally bumping elbows and knees, swapping human warmth and lunch breath.

Unlike the faded beige scheme of the rest of the lab, the coffee-and-milk color of the walls, the cinderblock walls here are painted a pale blue. It gives the space an indefinable, open and airy feel, enhanced by the sunlight pouring in through two large east-facing windows. Maybe you don't notice the color explicitly; but you feel the difference as soon as you walk in.

The office technically has two entrances, but one is blocked off with a table and never used. The functioning entrance—the door with the copulating gods—is almost always open. The whole lab has an open-door policy. We never close our office doors except at night when we leave, or for the occasional private phone call. The reason for the openness must be Charlie's immense and inclusive personality, which has rubbed off on the rest of us. We often spend our time sitting in his office talking to him, or ransacking his file cabinets looking through photocopied papers, or arguing with each other during lab meetings. The weekly meetings help hold the social fabric of the lab together.

The furniture in Charlie's office is a collection of miscellaneous lab stools and office chairs, variously green, orange, dirty white or sky blue, sometimes sticky on your legs where the vinyl upholstery has been repaired with duct tape. The diversity of color gives almost a carnival feel to the room, or maybe like the yurt of a Mongolian chief. The chairs are packed so close around the edges of the room that the arms and wheels clunk and catch against each other. The floor is covered by a rug, the only one in the lab, burgundy red with black and white geometric designs and a knotted, white, string fringe that has gone gray with age and dirt.

The room has a chalkboard mounted on the wall. I guess it's there in case anyone wants to draw an idea during a lab discussion, but it's old and speckled, and its aluminum tray contains only broken bits of chalk and a layer of thick gray chalk dust. Having been hit by the hard backs of too many chairs, the tray is loose and beginning to break away from the rest of the chalkboard.

A little projection screen, about two feet across, is fixed to a different wall. Sometimes the screen is used by students when they give practice talks, but more often, Charlie shows slides from his latest trip around the world. He likes to show landscapes and mountains, temples and trees, and colorful people. The projection screen is one of those old-fashioned, pull-down gizmos, but the spring mechanism malfunctioned years ago and now the thing won't stay in the down position no matter how hard you pull the handle. Typical of our makeshift lab, Charlie solves the problem by hanging a hunk of metal on the handle, a 0.5 kg weight from an old-fashioned scale, tied on with a bit of green insulated electrical wire and clipped in place with a small-sized surgical hemostat. A mountaineering pick from Nepal, made of weathered, grainy wood and rusty iron, a souvenir from one of his trips, leans in the corner under the projection screen.

Framed on the east wall between the two windows, one of Charlie's photos shows a farm woman from East Asia, a close-up of her upper body in half profile. She's wearing what looks like a red felt shirt and a gray cloth wrapped around her head. Her country is unclear. Her face is chiseled, with black eyebrows and piercing eyes—a striking photo. Another framed photo shows a row of young monks in training, six-year-old boys shaved and sitting cross-legged in orange robes.

Visually, the room is dominated by four tall, cobalt-blue, metal file cabinets, about five feet high, two on each side of the room. They contain Charlie's collection of scientific reprints, often with bits of paper sticking out from imperfectly closed drawers. The slide projector sits on top of one file cabinet. On top of another, hovering over everyone's heads, stands an antique, steel-and-brass balance, in a glass display case. One of its metal weights has been used to fix the projection screen. I believe the vintage scale was a gift from one of Charlie's own mentors, years ago, although I never got the whole story.

The dark brown, faux-wood surface of Charlie's desk is usually cluttered with a Macintosh computer, a pile of books, the yellow legal pads on which Charlie always writes his lecture notes, a big metal yogurt spoon, a metal cup with a welded handle that he uses for water, a hand-crafted leather mug with a supply of pencils leaning out of it, a white cardboard soup pint from Cox's deli leaving oily chicken-soup rings on the surface of the desk, a leather book satchel that looks something like a saddle bag, and his little red memorandum book that he calls his mind, strapped closed with a rubber band. If he misplaces the memorandum book, he stumps around the lab plaintively saying, "I lost my mind. Did anyone see my mind?"

Four long bookshelves are fixed to the wall immediately to the right of the desk. They are made of varnished, brown, wooden planks on steel brackets, and contain rows of black-bound theses, the intellectual offerings of many previous graduate and undergraduate students, as well as Charlie's own graduate thesis from Harvard, bound in green cloth. On the rest of the shelf space, in no order, Charlie has stuffed a miscellany of books, the old color-coded abstract volumes from the Society for Neuroscience, a collection of past Charlie minds in many colors, books on art, books on bizarre topics. For a long time, he has a college textbook on sexual practices in the US, with artists' illustrations. He has a book by Karen Horney on Feminine Psychology and a book by John Hughlings Jackson on neurology. Next to the books, acting as something of a bookend, sits a 1960's boxy, brown radio, with a long trailing wire as an antenna. It's usually tuned to a classical station.

The two tables in the office are surfaced in cheap Formica,

one silver-gray and one dark brown, the thin layer of Formica peeling off at the edges and showing a reddish granular layer of glue beneath. The skinny legs of the tables are chrome, old and spotted. The tables are often cluttered with cloth-bound library books, Xeroxed papers, enlarged photos from Charlie's travels, and strange objects brought back from exotic locations, like carved wooden masks from New Guinea dripping with ropey hair.

The windows flood the room with light. The venetian blinds are made of wide, off-white metal strips, grimy at the edges where they have probably never been cleaned. They're usually pulled up crookedly to the top of the window to let in the light, the dingy rope mechanism straggling down one side and spilling onto the table beneath. In good weather, when the windows are unlatched and hinged open, the chirping and warbling of sparrows and the occasional caw of a crow drift in with the subdued sounds of Princeton traffic or the hourly tolling of church bells from the corner a block away. Sometimes the branches of the rhododendron tree just outside the window shudder from a sudden squirrel. In summer, you can smell cut grass from the narrow verge under the window, or the strong dark odor of the woodchips, or the odor of rain and mud in the wet Princeton spring, or maybe that smell of fresh chicken soup just brought over from Cox's deli, seeping a little bit and soaking into the white paper bag. Usually the soup comes with two saltines in a plastic package, and Charlie tears open the package with his teeth and stuffs the crackers in his mouth, the crumbs scattering over his beard, shirt, and shorts.

During the lab meeting, Charlie sits at one end of the office, alternately hunched or sprawled in his wheeling desk chair, dragging it closer to us by a characteristic rowing movement of his feet across the rug. He takes up more space than anyone else, and not just because his personality is larger than life. He squirms and twitches so much that he needs the extra space. His deeply tanned arms and legs seem to go everywhere.

For about a year, he wore a necklace made of acorns. Then, for months, he wore his participation medal for the New York Marathon. He often wears a plaid, short-sleeved, button-down shirt with a breast pocket, the fabric tight over his barrel chest and the round of his stomach, tucked into a pair of elephant-colored shorts, with a braided leather belt, along with a pair of old, worn, warped, Birkenstock sandals on his otherwise bare feet. His toes are often glaringly bruised, the toenails crooked, from running marathons. We all politely try not to look at his feet.

His chair rattles every time he fidgets, crossing or uncrossing his legs, gesticulating, looking startled at someone's comment, making a vigorous comment of his own, his bushy hair and beard vibrating, his dark-framed glasses glinting in the light from the window.

"Very good! Excellent, a real high-risk, high-yield experiment, see, now you're thinking creatively." Or, "Oh God, there's umpteen million experiments on that quantitative mash! Don't tell me you want to do one of those!" He's always strictly honest, his speech machinery wired directly to some genuine center, free with praise when he means it and willing to slit the throat of an idea when he feels it deserves slitting. He's always self-deprecating but never modest. He's full of emotional vibrancy, a potent psychological immediacy, even when talking about a minor technical feature of a scientific paper or about the quality of the soup or about a Fellini film he just saw or about a book review he just read. When he makes a point, he often reaches forward in a characteristic way, his hand shaking slightly with eagerness, not with a forefinger extended in a stereotypical "hear my point" gesture but instead with his fingers slightly curled as if he's a large monkey reaching for a small cookie. When he laughs, it's a surprisingly quiet, asthmatic laugh given his normally booming voice, but he's so invested in the laugh that sometimes tears come out and he has to take off his glasses and wipe his eyes with a multicolored, tie-dyed handkerchief that he pulls out of his pocket. I can still hear him and see him so vividly, sitting in his chair and talking to us, that I think I never left that lab meeting.

22

TIRIN'S OFFICE

It used to be Seamus's office. A rhododendron tree grows outside, shading the window. Irritated at the tree, Seamus takes a wood saw from our shop room, goes outside, and cuts down the biggest branch. That's a can-do attitude. Then he feels guilty, or maybe decides that, like George Washington with the cherry tree, he can't tell a lie, and gives himself up to the department manager. Bernie screams at him and tells him that he's culpable for damaged property. It doesn't pay to be George Washington in today's world.

Later, it's Paul Azzopardi's office. Charlie makes a discovery. Feeling hungry one day, when no one's looking, he sneaks into Paul's office and scrounges in the desk drawers. He finds a giant chocolate bar, the good kind, a European brand with a high cocoa content, the wrapper already opened, and he breaks off a few squares. Just a few, of course. The next day, he's drawn to the same secret cache. Every few days, he sneaks back in and steals a few more squares. Eventually, he begins to wonder how the chocolate bar has lasted so long. It's eternally regenerating, like a salamander losing its tail. It's a puzzle, but not enough to distract him from eating the chocolate. Months go by, and finally he grows careless in his stealth-craft and is caught in the act. Embarrassed, he confesses and explains that he only intended to sneak a few squares now and then until the bar was gone. But it never ran out, so he never stopped. Paul A finds the episode hilarious. "That was twenty bars!" he says. "I wondered why I had to buy a new one every three days. I couldn't figure out how I was eating so much chocolate!"

For a while it's Colombo's office, before he moves into mine. Then Xintian sits there, as does Katsuki, Chaoui, Zhang, and Hillary. But I think of it as Tirin's office because he occupies it for the last many years of the lab.

One day, sitting at his desk, Tirin leans back a little too far and the chair flips. The wheels slip out from underneath and the chair crashes on its back. Tirin lies on the floor, immobile, his head against the tan floor tiles, his arms outstretched. Nina, the lab tech who sits in the histology room across the hall, sees the accident and runs over in horror. With her experience as a paramedic, she's convinced that he's dead because he isn't moving. He must have fractured the back of his skull.

But when she reaches his side, he looks mildly up at her. "Interesting!" he says. "I've never looked at the room from this perspective before. I don't think I've ever looked at the ceiling."

23

THE KITCHEN AND THE SHOP

For a few weeks, we have a terrible fruit fly infestation. Someone left peaches in the kitchen for too long, and the flies spontaneously generated. Even after the peaches are gone, the flies won't leave. They infiltrate every part of the lab, even my office sixty feet down the hall.

Always a creative thinker, Tirin devises a plan. He chops an apple into fine pieces, heats it on a dish in the kitchen microwave to generate an attractive aroma, and then opens the microwave door. Hundreds of fruit flies swarm inside and cluster on the cooked apple pieces. Sneaking up, Tirin slams the door shut and microwaves the flies to death. All is fair in love and war—but, alas, the maneuver barely makes a dent in the population. Eventually, we discover that by drying every bit of water from the sink with paper towels, plugging the drain, and leaving the kitchen unused for a week, we can prevent the creatures from finding enough moisture to breed, and the problem is solved.

The kitchen and shop share a room at the end of the hall. The kitchen area occupies the left side of the room, as you look in the door, and the shop occupies the right side. The juxtaposition of kitchen and shop is typical of us. I'm guessing it's a safety hazard to have a kitchen contaminated by shop debris—sawdust, metal filings, lead solder.

Many a time, Tirin, Charlotte, and I have dinner in the kitchen-shop, when we're too lazy or poor to splurge at Theresa's Italian restaurant. Dinner is when we argue about our experiments and presidential politics, movies and social trends, monkeys and people in the department. Lunch is also when we argue. So is every other time we're together. We're always litigating some case to each other, and the unspoken rule is that whoever can push an argument to the edge of comic absurdity, without going too far, wins.

We wheel the aluminum cart out from its space between the sink and the fridge, cover it with a blue surgical pad as an elegant tablecloth, and spread out whatever feast is available. Steak cooked in the scummy electric pan. Chicken souvlaki on pita from Zorba's Greek Takeout. Chinese garlic pork and noodles from the fish-and-chips restaurant. The fish-and-chips takeout restaurant down the street is run by a Chinese family, and one day as I'm waiting for my order, I notice a Chinese customer ordering from a secret, folded-up, hand-written menu. I ask to see the secret menu, but it's written in Chinese. With some negotiation and translation, I manage to order secret food, and it's the best Chinese food you can get in Princeton. At least, the garlic pork noodles are.

We scrub up some bent metal forks and spoons from the cluttered dish drainer, pour some wine, and set everything nicely on the fuzzy absorbent tablecloth that looks like a giant diaper. We use proper ceramic plates, white with a blue willow pattern, that Charlie donated to the lab decades ago. They're chipped around the edges. One of us might sit on a lab stool, perched high, hunched over the cart. Another might sit on an office chair with wheels, rather low. It doesn't matter—we eat together, drink, lick our plates like savages, clean up, more or less, which partly involves turning the disposable tablecloth into a sack of trash and cramming it into the nearby metal garbage can. Then we return to our data and equipment for the rest of the long evening. Or we watch a movie on Tirin's computer in his office.

In the shop half of the room, we can build or repair almost anything. We've all fixed lamps and tables for our houses. My workmanship is crude but practical. I lock a piece of wood in the vice, nail a thing to a thing, solder this to that, slap on some duct tape, and I'm done. It works. Other people are more delicate and spend hours aesthetically refining a project until it could be sold in a store.

When you first walk in the door of the room, directly to your right you'll see the gray metal side wall of a tool cabinet rising almost to the height of the ceiling. The light switch for the room is, peculiarly, mounted on the side of that tool cabinet, wired through a brown plastic track that rises up the cabinet and disappears into a hole cut in the ceiling tile. I've never before seen the main light switch of a room detached from the wall and fixed, instead, to the side of a piece of furniture, and I am fascinated by that choice. Whatever important goal I have in mind when I walk into the shop, whatever hammer or wrench or Pop-Tart I'm here to fetch, sometimes I like to put my task aside for a moment and think about the strangeness of this particular detail. Years ago, when the lab was first built, somebody must have arranged the furniture, putting a workbench here, a shelf there, and then stood back, arms akimbo, and said, "Gosh, this tool cabinet and that light switch are not compatible. I can move the cabinet to another part of the room, or I can pry the light switch off the wall and screw it onto the side of the cabinet." It bespeaks a level of creativity, an emancipation from functional fixity, a kind of four-dimensional problem solving that is the essence of Charlie's lab.

I know that men and tools have a stereotyped relationship. Little boys love their toy hammers, and grown men still maintain their childish amusements. I don't think I ever had that type of wow-it's-so-cool relationship to tools. I grew up around them on a farm, so to me they're just things that you need. But I notice that tools do have a peculiar way of attaching themselves to memory. I remember individual tools like I remember the pets I grew up with. I think the reason is that you interact with them physically. They're not just something you see or hear or read about; you hold them in your hands and do stuff with them. When a specific tool is gone forever, lost decades ago, your brain can never quite believe it's gone because your hands still know exactly how to grasp it, how much force you need to lift it, and what its texture feels like in your palm. I remember the wooden handle of the grub hoe on my parents' farm and the feel of the large yellow bow saw. Just so, the drawer of Allen wrenches in Charlie's lab must still exist—it has to—because I know exactly what it feels like to pull out that gray steel drawer, hold it in my hands, experience its specific weight, and put it down on top of the work surface to root for the particular black metal Allen wrench that I need. The memory has too much physicality to be a ghost.

The tool cabinet, made of dark gray steel, is about seven feet tall and perhaps two feet deep and is incredibly heavy, as I know from trying to move it. The raw steel bottom has cut into the soft, linoleum material of the floor tiles, giving the cabinet a permanent footprint. If you enter the room and turn around to face the cabinet, you'll see that its bottom third is occupied by an open shelf on which spools of colorful electrical wire are stacked. The top third is dominated by a plywood-lined alcove with tools hanging on hooks. Between those two segments, the middle third of the cabinet is filled with little drawers. Each gray metal drawer has a tag holder on its front surface, into which you can slide a labeled piece of paper. Somebody must have labelled every draw years ago, but by now most of the tags are gone. The few remaining labels don't match what's in the drawers.

Every member of Charlie's lab eventually learns exactly what kind of item can be found in which drawer. Second row down, second from the right, that's where you'll find the Allen wrenches. Here's a drawer with alligator clips. A drawer with banana connectors. A drawer with glass lenses. A drawer with wood screws. A drawer with metal screws. A drawer with many long iron files and hacksaw blades. A drawer with subdivisions for bolts, nuts, and washers. A drawer with electrical connectors that have twelve or more pins. A drawer with sandpaper. A drawer with small electric fans for cooling hot equipment. A drawer with metal lab-ware for holding flasks and Bunsen burners.

To survive in the lab, you need to remember where everything is located, like a squirrel that remembers where all its nuts are cached. There's no organization, no system, and you must build a detailed mental map. If you need a retinoscope, you must know immediately to look in the top, right drawer of the prep room, in a particular white cardboard box. If you need spare pieces of Plexiglas or Lexan to make a new chair part, you must look in the bottom two drawers, beneath the counter, in the awake room. If you need formaldehyde for a specimen, go to the metal cabinet next to the sink in the histology room. The electric drill—the big, gray, metal drawer beneath the wooden workbench in the shop. Sheer necessity is why I retain such a detailed knowledge of which drawers contain which items. That kind of memory is what binds you to a place, like strings attaching specific pieces of your brain to specific external locations, so that even when the place is gone, it survives forever in that pattern of anchor points in your brain.

The dominating presence in the shop is a massive wooden workbench on gray metal legs. The tabletop is a two-inch-thick slab of unfinished wood, a good three feet deep and six feet wide, filling up the available space on the south wall. The surface is splattered with black paint from past projects, scarred and cut, full of drill holes and saw marks. From where the surface is cut, you can see that the slab is made of a dense particleboard. If you look in the indentations, the partial drill holes, you're likely to find little round balls of used solder that rolled in and got stuck.

We've all spent hours of our lives in front of that shop table, a hacksaw or a drill in hand, a piece of Plexiglas or Lexan or wood firmly in the big iron vice, often with a surgical towel pinched in there to prevent the iron from scratching the piece we're shaping. Carpentering is a meditative experience. It's slow, careful, thoughtful, but for all the thought and planning, it also gives you an opportunity to clear everything from your mind. It's calming. Your clothes are covered in little crunchy bits of plastic from cutting Lexan. The floor crunches under your shoes. The smell of partly melted plastic, or of drilled metal, or of cut plywood, suggests that some unhealthy particles are probably contaminating your lungs.

At the back of the work table, you may find the blue plastic tray in which we keep the solder and the soldering iron. The iron has a blue-and-black plastic handle. I know it well. I've had many encounters with it. As careful as I try to be, I burn myself almost every time I use it. The problem with soldering is that your attention is focused on the delicate copper pins of a multi-prong connector, not on the hot iron toward which you are reaching under peripheral vision. Charlie says that the best way to test the worth of your students is to make them wire up a Jones plug—one of those connectors with thirty-two or sixty-four pins crowded into a tiny space. Your students may not succeed, but if they lose their minds and smash the plug with a hammer, then you know they lack the mental fortitude to be scientists. I've never wired up a sixty-four-pin connector, but I've managed thirty-two pins. It's all about meditation. It has nothing to do with technical expertise or engineering cleverness, and you don't need to know anything about circuits—it's a mental art form. It's calming and lovely, until you burn your fingers again on the soldering iron.

I love the diversity of work in the lab. Everyone here must be a passable carpenter, electrician, equipment designer, computer programmer, monkey trainer, vet, brain surgeon, janitor, data analyst, writer, graphic artist, debater, teacher, and public speaker. Every day you move effortlessly from one domain to another. You're never bored but at the same time can never feel satisfied with your current level of skill. Neuroscience is a game of continual skill accumulation.

24

THE LAST LITTLE ROOM

I have only one room left to describe to you. It's the smallest room in the lab, hidden in the back-most part of the warren, tucked behind the shop, its doorway next to and partly blocked by the workbench. The door doesn't even close all the way, especially with spare cables and lab coats draped over the top of it. We sometimes don't even see it as a door to another room, so much as a convenient "thing" holder. I don't know the original purpose of that little cell of a room, but when we enter it at all, we treat it as a closet. If you ever wanted to play hide-and-seek in the lab, it would be the place to hide, farthest from anyone's spatial consciousness.

As you look in the door, you'll see that the room is like the cell of a medieval monk: tiny, windowless, closed in by dingy beige concrete on all sides. A metal cabinet contains rows of old brains floating in jars. In the farthest back of the room, a black wooden table is wedged into the tight space. The table is empty except for a very dusty lab beaker with some old, whitish, dried residue at the bottom. It could be dried-up bits of brain—literally, memory dust. Somebody must have used the beaker years ago and accidentally left it. The purpose of the beaker, the purpose of the table, and the purpose of the room are lost. Brain dust and a forgotten beaker in an unused room: a metaphor for science past.

25

EXODUS

I don't want to write this chapter. I'll make it brief.

The regulators eventually catch up to us. The whole lab is condemned as a giant health hazard. On walk-through tours, men with suits and clipboards look with horror. Where did they come from? What unpleasant agency? The place is stacked with ancient dusty equipment, it's a confusing rabbit warren of rooms that could trap you in a fire, the ceilings are too low and the corridors too narrow, choking-hazard wires hang everywhere connecting equipment to equipment, the floors are not made of modern material, and the monkeys and humans are chaotically intermingled. Is it really true that the monkeys are wheeled through the lunchroom? That part can't possibly be true. It must be a joke. Look at the confused outrage on their faces. They want something new, shiny, standardized, like a lab in a TV show. They want something photogenic. They want professionalism, modernism, and top-down regulation. The popular design concept, nowadays, is all about shared spaces instead of private labs, open benches instead of sequestered rooms, plastic equipment instead of dusty metal and wood, so that everything is washable and sterilizable, countable, modular, disposable, replaceable, photographable, and brochureable.

It's September 2002.

Like refugees expelled from the homeland, we file out the front door of the ruined, empty lab, holding cardboard boxes and pushing carts, carrying the few belongings that are modern enough, plastic enough, cleanable enough, that we are allowed to keep them. We're on our way to a relocation project in another part of the building that can never be a home and can never truly be ours. The old lab has become so much a part of me, a natural extension of my body image, that I feel like my arms and legs have been amputated. Slick, plastic, artificial limbs are being offered by eager salesmen.

I don't want to describe the new place, where the spirit of the lab dies, because I don't want to contaminate my portrait of the old. I prefer to leave Charlie's lab poised in eternal stasis. I'll close my eyes for a moment and put myself back, as vividly as I can, to a place that has been gone for twenty years, and by effort of will I'll try to make it come back again.

It's noon. Charlie is in his office, shouting editorial instructions to Maida, their Brooklyn duet booming through the lab. Hugo is in the colony feeding the monkeys, who are collectively hooting and rattling their cages in high spirits over lunch. Nina is in the histology room, on the phone ordering equipment, yelling at a supplier who made a mistake, while multitasking and timing a chemical reaction, her electronic stopwatch beeping every minute and a half. Dylan is in his over-large, flapping white lab coat, wheeling The Mole down the corridor, past my open office door. The Mole, in his plastic chair on his metal cart, his collar holding him to the chair, is swiveling around, closely watching everything, baring his impressive, two-inch canines at anyone bold enough to make eye contact. Tirin is in his experiment room, rewiring his equipment, blasting Spin Doctors. I know he's hopping from foot to foot as he reaches for a tool here and a wire there, performing the science dance. I'm in my office, sitting in my green padded chair, slumped down, feet stretched under the desk until I'm almost horizontal, my hands up on the keyboard, trying to phrase the introduction to a scientific paper. I've been working all morning and have written only a couple paragraphs. It's sunny outside. It's June. The church bells toll midday. Charlie comes out of his office, stumping through the corridor saying, "Lunch? Lunch? What about lunch? Hey? Hoo? Anyone?"

Michael S. A. Graziano is a professor of neuroscience and psychology at Princeton University. He is also a writer, composer, and occasional ventriloquist. He is the author of many books (both novels and neuroscience books), and has written for *The Atlantic*, *The New York Times*, *The Wall Street Journal*, and other media outlets. His research at the Princeton Neuroscience Institute has spanned topics from movement control to how the brain processes the space around the body. His current work focuses on the brain basis of consciousness.